CREATING FORMAL GARDENS

CREATING
FORMAL GARDENS

ROY STRONG

Little, Brown and Company
Boston · Toronto · London

For Rosemary Verey, my Garden Muse

Amongst the many people who have inspired and contributed
to the making of this book, I would particularly like to
express my gratitude to Gill Tomblin for vizualizing
my designs exactly as I saw them in my mind's eye. R.S.

First U.S. edition

ISBN: 0-316-81924-7

Library of Congress Catalogue Card No. 89-80488

First published in 1989 in the United Kingdom by
Conran Octopus Limited.

10 9 8 7 6 5 4 3 2 1

PRINTED IN SPAIN

Half title and title: A re-created Tudor knot at
an earlier and a later stage.

Contents page: An inspiration to all those who wish to
create a small formal garden.

CONTENTS

THE
LANGUAGE
OF FORMALITY

I have always been in love with formal gardens. It is a passion fed not only by the reality of those which survive from the past but perhaps even more by those lost gardens which are recorded in the hundreds of paintings and engravings from the sixteenth and seventeenth centuries. Of all forms of topographical art, that which depicts the formal garden at its apogee in the age of *Le Roi Soleil* provides the most delectable imaginary walks. How delightful it is to join a gentleman in a curled wig and a lady in an elaborate head-dress, strolling along an allée bordered with clipped obelisks of yew, following them into a hidden cabinet of treillage where a single jet of water shoots upwards into the air from a gilded fountain figure. There are gracious terraces on which to parade where orange trees grow in huge terracotta pots and steps lead down to the parterre — an amazing composition, its green box hedges cut to form some fantastic arabesque pattern. There may be a grotto to visit, a maze in which to lose oneself or a wilderness to wander through. Yet even as one is falling under the enchantment of these old formal gardens, one cannot help realizing how full they are of gardening ideas and traditions which we today have either totally lost or simply forgotten.

Surprisingly one is often struck by their unexpected simplicity. Frequently a very large and grand garden would consist of little more than symmetrically placed areas of grass with a few trees trained to shape; but the delineation of those areas of grass and the placing of those trees would be achieved in such a way as to guarantee year-round satisfaction unimpaired by the changing seasons. Equally, a wilderness (then, a formal garden less wild than the name suggests) must have been a refreshing feature — a plantation in which to walk or sit, with 'rooms' formed by hedges, and groves often planted with little flowering trees or sweet-smelling honeysuckle and roses. Avenues of trees trained as mopheads but joined at ground level by a low hedge must also have been a beguiling garden feature, as indeed must have been a line of trees forming an arched palisade like an arcade in front of a building or around a cloister. Using many such devices, these gardens make a clear welcome division between the world of untamed nature beyond their magical confines and that of nature subdued by the powers of art practised within them. Viewed from above they would appear carved out of the landscape, oases of elegance and beauty holding at bay the barbarism beyond.

◀ My own formal garden. In 1974 this was a field for cattle. By 1987 it looked like this. Steps made in the slope provide a spectacular entrance.
▲ The tranquillity and charm of a simple formal arrangement, a small, evergreen and easily maintained incident in a much larger garden.

I think that the key to a formal garden's appeal to the eye and imagination is perhaps the awareness that nothing in it is ever random. Everything is always there for a reason, so that the removal of even one feature immediately shatters the perfect balance of the parts. One of the reasons for this resides in the fact that the elements which make up such a garden — although generally the same as those deployed in any other style of gardening — are used with a special and distinctive emphasis. We have forgotten how recent is the enormous dependence on plants. Plant introductions reached a peak during the last century, but until then even the most celebrated gardens had been created with a relatively restricted repertory. Much greater emphasis was given to the other elements which made up the garden picture, above all its permanent features, whether built or natural. In the early formal periods a garden was admired as much for its gravel walks, clipped hedges and topiary, statuary and use of water as for any seasonal luxuriance.

Descriptions of gardens abound which contain no reference at all to flowers, the ingredient now generally prized above all others; and yet, at the time, these gardens were regarded as giving total satisfaction.

The formal garden, with its very strong emphasis on the importance of structure, stemmed from a belief that the garden was something which was to be visited and appreciated through every season of the year, whose appeal was never to rest solely on a few summer months of abundant bloom. The spell of a formal garden resides instead in a perfect placing of unchanging features in utter harmony with each other. Being architectural in concept, its pleasure to the eye is exactly parallel to that of a perfectly proportioned building. A formal garden continues to bring pleasure even in winter frost and under snow. It is then, for example, that its hedges come into their own, defining space; the exact proportions of that space and the height and cut of that hedge will have been carefully conceived from the outset.

The same principles apply to another twelve-month ingredient, evergreen topiary; the changing effects of light and shade and shadow through the months on those living architectural elements will always be thrilling. Well placed sculptural features will likewise provide garden delight and spectacle in all weathers and at all times of the year.

In the planning of my own garden during the last fifteen years those early bird's-eye views of late seventeeth-century formal gardens have been a major influence. They are teeming with ideas for hedges and enclosures, ascents and descents, eye-catchers and view-points as well as for uses of topiary and the training of trees and plants. I was not in the least put off by the grandeur of some of the gardens; indeed, many were not grand at all — rather the reverse in fact, being nothing more than the re-ordering of nature with ruler and compasses in hand, to achieve an architectural effect which only needed seasonal mowing and an annual trim and prune. Certainly they can be far easier to

cope with than many gardens today in which the obsession with massive displays of flowers continues unabated.

This is, in fact, a point that seems to me to be crucial. Formal gardening has mistakenly acquired a bad name for itself as being labour-intensive, yet with foresight and good planning it can be exactly the opposite, offering ease of maintenance with maximum effect. Large size, again, is often seen as a prerequisite; but if one looks into those views of early gardens, one discovers that they are composed of a series of square and rectangular enclosures that are often quite small in dimension. Furthermore — and even more relevant — such enclosures are similar in shape and area to many present-day gardens.

These are the facts which prompted me to embark on the present book, for here surely, in the formal garden heritage, is the tradition most apposite for our own time; these are deeply satisfying gardens, often of remarkable simplicity, requiring low maintenance and

occupying space of the kind and shape that most people have to deal with. Let me add at once that this book is in no way a plea for historical revivalism (although that option is open as the reader will discover) but rather the contrary, a plea for a rediscovery and re-invention of the tradition in the modest terms of the small gardens of the late twentieth century.

The tradition of formal garden-making is, of course, not a dead one. In some countries the tradition is more vigorous than in others. In England it remains strongest in what can conveniently be categorized as the country-house tradition, where the basis for design continues to be the famous compromise evolved during the early years of this century by the architect Sir Edwin Lutyens and the plantswoman Gertrude Jekyll in which a strong architectural articulation of a site is softened by a lush planting that breaks into, but does not upset, the structural lines of the formality. The English formal tradition is weakest in the design

of public spaces, and also in the handling of small private gardens. Here, in the 1950s, the influence of the Brazilian Burhle Marx and the American Thomas Church, combined with a revival of interest in the English eighteenth-century landscape tradition, resulted in the miniaturization of the gracious splendour of a vast landscape park into the confines of the average rectangular suburban garden. The

THE DELIGHTS OF THE SEASON
The same garden in summer and in winter demonstrates the year-round pleasure to be had from the formal garden.

◀◀ In summer the greens are fresher and the palette range is extended by flowers, here in pink and white, using begonias, impatiens, roses, and in the pots, petunias.

▼ In winter the accent is on the architectural and sculptural form, hedges and topiary, under the play of light aided by the dramatic change of the hornbeam hedging to russet.

TYPES OF FORMALITY

◀ Yesterday. This traditional formal garden, with its box parterre, was laid out in 1875.

▲ Today. The same principles have resulted in this very different but equally formal garden which is purely of our own time.

outcome has rarely been successful and it is difficult to see any future for this kind of design.

The English dilemma is worth dwelling upon for a moment because, ever since the advent of landscape movement in the eighteenth century, England has continued to lead the world in its passion for gardening, and in what might be described as the garden debate. Almost all the main literature on contemporary garden design is English, and both the good and the bad sides of English design have proliferated throughout the English-speaking world, in the United States and the countries of the Commonwealth: Canada, Australia and New Zealand. The influence does not end there, for English gardening books are on sale in most bookshops in the English-reading northern European countries: the Netherlands, Germany and Scandinavia. Everywhere one travels one sees the twin influences of the Lutyens-Jekyll tradition and of the miniaturization of the landscape park. No other country, therefore, has had such an enormous impact on gardening. It is sad but true that Italy, the fount of the

formal tradition in the Renaissance, has little indigenous garden-design literature. Although many great formal gardens still exist there, the tradition of formal garden-making has lost much of its impetus.

It is encouraging to contrast this with the state of the tradition in the Netherlands where, although weakened, it retains a particular vigour. Some of the most stunning small gardens in the formal manner that are included in this book are Dutch, and the greatest re-creation of a Baroque formal garden — that of King William III at Het Loo, Apeldoorn — was undertaken by the Dutch in the 1970s. Dutch nurseries in the Boskoop area are still capable of supplying ready-trained topiary epitomizing a skill to all intents and purposes dead elsewhere.

There are, however, already increasing signs of a general revival of interest in the formal treatment of small areas, a movement recognized in some recent British garden writing. One of the pointers to the renewal is the fact that we are living in an era of what might be described as the 'decorator's garden'.

Everywhere we see the effect of the craze for interior decoration spreading out into the garden. A generation that rediscovered for itself the lost art of using wallpaper borders, curtain cutting and draping, marbling, dragging and stippling paint, besides a hundred other tricks, has begun to extend that interest to the techniques of topiary and plant-training, to the uses of treillage and garden statuary (sales of which by the leading salerooms are now a regular occurrence), to varieties of paving and pots, and to features such as the parterre and the ornamental kitchen garden, the potager. The interest has been strengthened by the recent explosion of enthusiasm for garden visiting and tours which has made an ever-wider public aware of some of the great gardens of the past.

There is at last some recognition that as a direct result of the last twenty-five years of an increasingly sterile informality, a vital part of our garden heritage has been lost. Awareness of this has been stimulated during the last decade by factors such as the development in Europe and the United States of garden history as a

TYPES OF FORMALITY

◀◀ Access passage. A simple connecting pathway transformed by framing hedges, borders planted with herbaceous perennials, and a trellis pergola.

◀ Town front garden. Formality as a crisply elegant solution to a perennial problem: a straight path up to the front door and box-edged symmetrical beds of tulips and pansies.

In other words, the area immediately around the house should be subject to the same type of treatment as the house itself. For many people that will be true already, for the small gardens of this century almost invariably have their boundaries defined in terms of a series of straight lines, usually forming a rectangle of some sort. That fact alone vitiates the attempt to transform the space within into a miniature landscape park. What it calls for is exactly the reverse — the reinforcement of the architectural structure and a design which successfully links the house with its surroundings. The formal tradition does precisely that, because it always works from the premise of boundaries.

Formality involves first and foremost the application of geometry at the planning stage. Just as the interior of a house is divided into rooms or areas, each for a particular function, so should the garden site be disposed. A plan for a formal garden begins by regularizing the space available — whatever its size or shape — working outwards from the house's doors and windows, both upstairs and down. This will govern the siting of paths and hedges, and the division of the area according to use, be it vegetable or flower garden, terrace or pond.

Implicit in the planning of a garden, as it is in the design of a building, is the importance of proportion. In the three centuries that followed the Renaissance, correct proportion was quantifiable and the construction of buildings and gardens was governed by codified rules and ratios which is why we continue to be struck by their total harmony today. Even though such rules no longer exist, an aesthetic sense of proportion is still crucial to the success of any major building or garden scheme. The best way to acquire this is to study architecture — particularly domestic houses — of pleasing proportions, noting the overall scale and the relationship of details such as windows and arches. These will help to give you vital clues to the structure of your garden.

The majority of the designs in this book have been devised for what a great number of people have: modest rectilinear areas that jut out at the front or back of a house. Some sites, however, are irregular and these are obviously more liable to occur in a non-urban environment where a house or cottage is often placed on a triangular or an L-shaped piece of land, sometimes with the added complication of sharp changes of level. In this case the most important thing to do is to impose geometry on the area by defining formal rooms and axes. Then you can either disguise the irregularities by filling in the remaining spaces or — as an attractive alternative — use them to heighten and emphasize

serious academic discipline. This has brought with it a burgeoning literature that has included reprints of the garden classics of the past, many of which deal with the formal garden. In addition, the plethora of recent illustrated books on gardens has made the formal heritage better known to a more general public.

Re-creations of historic gardens — most of those conserved date from before 1720 and are, therefore, formal in character — provide valuable touchstones. In Britain such re-creations owed much of their impulse to the National Trust which, during the 1960s and 1970s, undertook the reinstatement of a whole series of historic formal gardens. In the United States the restoration, begun in the 1920s, of the formal gardens of the early eighteenth century in Virginia, particularly those at Williamsburg, drew attention to the distinctive American contribution to the formal heritage. In France the restoration of gardens such as the Potager du Roi at Versailles and the re-creation of a vast Renaissance château garden at Villandry have given similar impetus to the revival of formality

in a country where the tradition has been far stronger and more pervasive than elsewhere.

The lessons of history are always relevant. In garden-making, as in all other arts, one goes back to go forward. We go to the past not to live in it but to create a future. Now is the moment to argue for a new inventiveness within the old formal tradition: a vitality based not on a nostalgia, but on an understanding of those principles which have governed the planning of formal gardens since they were first enunciated in the middle of the fifteenth century.

The formal treatment of gardens ought perhaps to be called the architectural treatment of gardens, for it consists in extending the principles of design which govern the house to the grounds which surround it. The object of all formal gardening is primarily to bring the two into harmony, to make the house seem to grow out of its surroundings. It is always possible to control the space around a house so as to bring nature into harmony with the building, but it is almost impossible to do the reverse and bring the house into harmony with nature.

the formality by the contrast of naturalistic planting. This achieves precisely the effect of those seventeenth-century gardens where the demarcation between the worlds of art and nature always provided an extra frisson of pleasure.

Once the basic geometry and proportions have been worked out, the design of a formal garden depends upon the implementation of three basic concepts: symmetry, perspective and pattern. Most fundamental is the handling of symmetry to achieve a harmonious balance of parts. This can be as simple as placing two Versailles tubs containing standard bay trees on either side of an entrance; or it can be as elaborate as focusing a whole garden with a central axis on a box parterre which is itself laid out as two halves of a pattern that exactly mirror each other. But pairing and mirror-imaging are only two obvious ways of engineering balance. A comparable effect can be arrived at by massing an even number of groups of trees and shrubs so that their form, foliage and shape will give overall contours which appear balanced to the onlooker's eye. The careful control of colour— such as in matching the tones and shapes but not the actual varieties of plants in two herbaceous borders — can also create a similar impression. Remember that empty space can play an important role in achieving balance in any composition.

Symmetry in gardening terms, therefore, can be set about in a number of ways. It should begin at the planning stage, with decisions about the disposition of the site, initially working outwards from the house and then looking backwards towards it. Studying the groundplans in this book (pages 102–145), one can see that the strongest of all statements in symmetrical ground-planning is making a path that links the house and garden into the central axis (see pages 104, 106, 112, 124, 128). That effect, if the garden is large, can be multiplied by further axes in different relations to the house and, if a series of garden rooms is possible, the permutations will be almost limitless. In one design (pages 114–16) the garden is divided into two unequal areas. Both have axes from the house, the main one to a little gazebo, a secondary one across a pond to an urn. But there are also symmetrical cross-axes: from a seat across the pond through yew buttresses to a statue, and from a simple arbour through the beds in a potager to the orchard beyond.

It is difficult to imagine a successful formal garden that is not articulated in at least one area by the symmetrical placing of geometrical shapes, whether circles, squares, rectangles or octagons. Any arrangement of beds in a mirror pattern, either halved or quartered, gives

powerful ground-level symmetry (pages 106, 118, 130). A potager (page 118) can be a quartered octagon resulting in four beds the same size at the centre; or it could be a succession of squares or triangles flanking a path (pages 114, 124). Even if the patterns within them vary, a pair of parterres of equal size will produce an effect of balance (pages 104, 108). So, too, will the division of grass into complementary sections of restful green (pages 112, 128). The concept of symmetry should also be applied to vertical elements of a formal garden — the hedges or any other devices, such as walls or fencing or trellis, which serve to divide and regulate the area. Hedges call for patience, but it will be abundantly rewarded: trained, clipped and pruned into perfect curves, crenellations or piers, they provide an unparalleled decorative effect which also enhances the symmetry of their position.

Pairing is the most obvious of all vertical devices. An avenue is an emphatic repetition of pairing and the longer it is the more emphatic it will be (pages 112, 117, 120). It doesn't have to be of trees; it could be of topiary or plants in terracotta pots (page 134). Buttresses are another device which create balanced recession, rather like wings on the stage of a Baroque theatre. These can, for example, be of

sombre yew, clipped into matching curlicues (page 114) or even treillage (page 132). Groups of four elements equidistant from each other can evoke an instant feeling of good order and tranquillity: four wooden obelisks supporting climbing roses (page 118), four flowering trees in the spandrels of a lawn (page 112) or arising from a more complex parterre (page 106), stone obelisks or terracotta pots at the corners of a parterre (pages 104, 108), even four fruit trees in a potager (page 114).

The formality of permanent features can be strengthened or softened according to the emphasis you wish to give your garden. Many people prefer to confine strict geometry to the basic structure and blur its lines with a luxuriant and even asymmetrical planting. The design for a Colonial American garden (page 106) offers a solution where the outer beds contain a mixed planting which tumbles over and breaks the rigid line of the composition. And the rich array of climbers in the tiny town garden (page 132) offsets what would otherwise be a somewhat austere stage set. On the other hand, the permanent formal structure can be emphasized rather than disguised by the planting. This is particularly clear in the case of parterres which depend on either bedding out or groundcover for their effect (pages 105, 106, 108, 130).

Symmetry exploits a disposition of space and a siting of artefacts in accordance with the principles of scientific single-point perspective. This was a Renaissance invention; the medieval optical tradition had been polycentric. The discovery of perspective quickly passed into the repertory of painting and theatre design and, by extension, into gardening. The invention was initially motivated by a desire to be able to site a building securely in the space of a picture. As a result, the understanding and application of the laws of perspective to building became an essential principle governing architecture itself and, as gardening was a branch of that art, garden design too. This mathematical ordering of space depends upon the notion that, from a single viewpoint, objects appear larger the nearer they are to the observer, and they diminish in size as they recede into the distance until they vanish at a single point on the horizon. Those principles governed the ordering of a picture's surface from the fifteenth century until the advent of this century, and still condition how we perceive the world around us.

The application of scientific perspective to garden planning effected a revolution. Without it we would have no ordering of space to lead the eye into the distance, no celebration of a garden's most ravishing view-points. Its rules governed formal garden-making in which space was arranged in terms of vistas linking house and garden and the various parts of the garden, for example by means of paths or avenues of trees. This simple formula of two parallel lines converging into the distance is basic to some of the most spectacular garden effects. Vista gives excitement and drama to the placing of the most important permanent artefacts in a garden's composition: summer houses, gazebos and seats (pages 106, 108, 114, 128, 134) as well as sculptural features such as sundials, statuary, urns and finials (pages 108, 110, 112, 128, 132). One really important object well placed in terms of perspective is more important than almost any other ingredient in the layout of a formal garden. In designing these gardens I was always acutely conscious that the removal of a focal object from the termination of a vista at once ruined the composition.

Vistas can be of a loose, almost informal kind achieved by a judicious planting scheme whereby colours and sizes of plants accentuate the distance, but usually they will be more explicitly emphasized by a path, a pergola, a tunnel, an arch or flanking hedges. They can be manipulated to enhance the optical illusion of distance. If, for example, instead of being strictly parallel, the edges of a vista are made to converge slightly, the distance from end to end

TYPES OF FORMALITY

▲◀ Country front garden. Verdant box hedging and a sundial give both order and style to what is otherwise a random planting.

▲ The potager. The practise of growing vegetables can be transformed into an art by formalizing the kitchen garden.

◀ Small back garden. A long narrow strip made intriguing by the creation of three separate contrasting areas, arranged symmetrically in perspective. Changes of level, hard and soft surfaces and water all help to give variety to a small area.

will seem greater than in fact it is. Equally, if you place a fairly small statue at a distance it will look further away than it really is until you get up close to it and realize that it is not as large as you thought. Rising ground also optically suggests far greater distance than is the reality. These kinds of optical effects can be exploited by the formal garden designer.

All framing devices depend upon perspective, whether you use a garden arch to focus the eye on something beyond it or plant trees and shrubs in such a way that they frame your view of the landscape. Perspective can also be accentuated by the use of colour. If we look into the distance, colour softens into a haze of greys and blues suggesting infinity. Strong colours, on the other hand — above all the reds — seem closer to us than they are. These are the basic principles of what is known as aerial perspective, which is an essential consideration in garden composition, and the planning of colour schemes for planting.

Pattern is likewise central to formal gardening. This must be borne in mind firstly for the hard surfaces, for their form and decoration can emphasize the geometric element of a design. A path or a paved area accentuates formality by the shape of its slabs, which can be elaborated further by lines of brick or cobbles (pages 109, 111, 113). A hard surface can even outline a false perspective to suggest greater distance in a restricted area (page 133). Remember that pattern in a garden is always deployed to greater effect if it can be looked down upon. This is why parterres are such ideal solutions for town houses with first floor living rooms (pages 129, 131). They utilize a time-honoured practice, and provide year-round enjoyment. Those who have a site which has changes of level really should plant some form of parterre (pages 102, 136), just for the sheer thrill of seeing it stretched out before them and then being able to descend into and through it. The steeper the descent the more dramatic and satisfying the effect will be.

Pattern can also be stressed by planting. In a formal garden every plant should be placed not only for its intrinsic beauty of colour, shape and form but as part of an overall scheme. A parterre filled with tulips in spring brings us the delight of the flowers themselves, but viewed from afar the tulips take on another role, as an integral part of a composition conceived in blocks of colour like a mosaic (pages 32–3). Victorian bedding schemes, of course, depended for their effect on pattern in planting (page 47). A rose garden in pink and white with borders of lavender, or potager beds planted in alternating rows of, say, ruby and green chard, are other

examples whereby pattern is seen to heighten formality.

In any given period there is a remarkable consistency in the kinds of patterns used in the decorative arts. This can be seen in textiles, book design, wallpapers, ceramics and furniture, for example, and also in gardens. An Elizabethan knot with its complex interlacing was a form of pattern one could find as easily on the sleeve of a dress as on the plasterwork of the ceiling of a long gallery. The swirling scrollwork in a Baroque parterre would be re-echoed in the marquetry of a veneered cabinet or on the fabric of a state bed. And we can move with ease from the Olde English gardens of the Arts and Crafts Movement to the wallpapers and textiles of William Morris.

Today we can still draw on the dressing-up box of the past — as all interior decorators do — but we can also draw on that of our own age. That is why I have based parterres on Art Deco textile, graphic and ceramic designs of the 1920s (page 131), and on Op Art and abstract painting of the 1960s (page 129). Whenever there is a visual culture which produces a repertory of decoration it can be translated into gardening terms. Do not be content with the designs I have suggested, but look around for your own ideas in books on twentieth-century art and design. You will be surprised at what can be adapted to the garden. Be bold and experiment; and do not live off re-cycling the past.

This seems to me to approach the true glory of the formal garden. Far from attempting the recreation of nature (idealized or bastardized, according to your point of view) as is generally the intention with informal gardens, the formal garden flourishes on artifice and confidently celebrates man's ability to control natural forces, imposing an order and creating forms that never exist in untouched nature. The imposition of such order begins with the actual planting of the trees and shrubs in circles and squares and rectangles and avenues. Some of its most stunning effects depend on the triumphant handling of plants into geometric and fantastic shapes at the whim of man, as we cut bays into standards, yew into cones and obelisks, clip box into scrolls and curves, or turn lime trees into airborne hedges. In doing that we are inheritors of a great tradition whose skills need to be revived with as much reverence as those of the other crafts that have been rescued during the last twenty years. Henceforward these skills will have to be learnt and passed on not by professional gardeners, as in the past, but by people who tend their own gardens. The formal garden is the garden as art, unashamedly presented as art to delight and enchant us.

TYPES OF FORMALITY

◀ Small town-house back garden. A very simple formal statement in greens in a strictly contemporary idiom of a kind which complements the architecture of the house to perfection.

▲ Small country-house garden. A delicate essay in the marriage of house and garden achieved through a traditional formal parterre. Even though the standard roses are protected by straw for the winter, the garden's strong architectural structure remains potent.

FORMAL ACCENTS

Formality can be a very fluid style of gardening. Even in an informal garden an accent of formality can be introduced to the composition. Here are some instances.

▲◀ Sentinels. A pair of topiary box shapes formalize an entrance in what is otherwise an informal border.

▲ Tableaux. A set piece of a bust on a plinth flanked by clipped pyramids gives form to a view into natural woodland.

◀ Hedges. The addition of a low clipped hedge around a tree immediately frames it with formality.

▲▶ Stilt hedges and pleaching. Lighter alternative to solid hedges still make strong formal statements in the garden.

▶ Contrast. Weeping roses given order by the insertion between them of evergreen screens like wings in a theatre.

THE PRINCIPLES OF
FORMALITY : SYMMETRY

Symmetry is one of the key means of bringing harmony and balance to a formal garden. It can be achieved in several ways.

◀ ▲ Trees. This simple symmetrical avenue of standard maples immediately strikes a note of ordered enticement.

◀◀ Ornament. Ornaments can be used to establish symmetry. Here a pair of finials flanking a flight of steps mirrors the pair of statues in the distance that mark the boundaries of the two gardens.

▲ Evergreens. Sculpted evergreens give year-round symmetry.

◀ Plants. The theme of the pair of upright yew obelisks is taken along the garden path by complementary plantings of lavender and *Alchemilla mollis*.

THE PRINCIPLES OF FORMALITY : VISTA

This prime ingredient of magic and allurement in a garden may be achieved in several ways.

◀ The tunnel. A vista may be contained and focused through enclosure, in this instance by training fruit trees over a frame.

▼ Colour. The blue spikes of delphiniums fill a pair of borders flanking a grass path leading to a fine gateway and another enclosure in the garden.

◀ Hedges and trees. A receding avenue of trees, trained as standards and with their branches creating a vault, and a hedge turning russet form a mysterious passage within a garden.

▼◀ Gates. These make wonderful terminations to a vista for they excite curiosity about what lies beyond. Here a glimpse may be seen through transparent ironwork.

▼ The back door. Few vistas are more important than the one which leads into the garden. Here an ornament glimpsed over water is framed by a beautiful planting of astilbes and hostas.

THE PRINCIPLES OF FORMALITY : PATTERN

Formal gardening has been a branch of the decorative arts through the centuries, and has always reflected changing styles of ornament. Nothing reveals this more clearly than the deployment of the shape and colour of plants to achieve distinctive pattern.

▲ Hedges. Low hedges, here of clipped box, are a means of obtaining year-round pattern emphasized by light and shade.

◀ Block planting. Geometrical beds—in this case a box parterre filled with the blue flowers of forget-me-nots—can be planted to make a strong statement in a single colour. The changes can be rung from year to year and season to season using plants, whether bulbs, annuals or bedding plants, which have a long flowering period.

▲ Flowers. Even without a containing structure flowers can be made into pattern through planting.

▲ ▶ Vegetables. The ordinary kitchen garden is tranformed by planting vegetables as pattern, like these lines of contrasting colour.

▲ Herbs. Frothy blue rue clipped to make a low serpentine hedge across a flowerbed makes up a different kind of pattern.

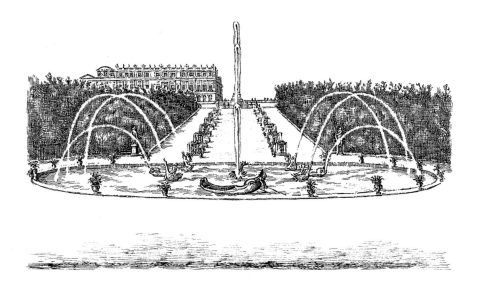

THE HERITAGE OF FORMALITY

The modern history of the formal garden in the modern period can be conveniently divided into two distinct historical phases, one before and one after the development of the landscape style. The first period runs from about 1450 to 1750 and grew directly out of the renaissance impulse to re-create the gardens of classical antiquity. It was in England that that phase first came to an end, when what we know as the landscape movement, under the aegis of William Kent (1685–1748) and subsequently of 'Capability' Brown (1716–1783), swept away the formal gardens of the Stuart age. The style later spread to the rest of Europe and the United States, particularly in the aftermath of the French Revolution and the Napoleonic wars.

The second period of formality in garden design was, perhaps surprisingly, a direct expression of the Romantic movement and sought its inspiration in the styles of the renaissance and baroque ages as much as the first had in antiquity. We are still living in that period. Its quintessence has been 'historical revivalism'—whether the early Victorians' desire to re-create the gardens of Tudor England or our own obsession with the pre-1914 country-house garden, which might almost be said to epitomize a revival of revivalism.

It is sad for those gardeners today who have an interest in re-creation that the small formal gardens of the past have not survived. Of the large-scale gardens designed for palaces and great country houses, a number still exist. In spite of the fact that they may have changed much over the centuries, their dependence on permanent structural features has meant that their essence still remains; and from that there is much to be learned, even for the most modest of gardens.

Too many people visit the famous formal gardens of the past in the belief that they have no relevance for us today with our minimal space and labour resources. But, paradoxically, in terms of sheer economy of effect such gardens are often immensely illuminating and they are the ideal place to look for and analyse those principles which have already been outlined as basic to formal design. It can be enormously valuable when visiting any of these gardens to spend a little time working out how the harmonious effect has been achieved and pinpointing what it is that gives particular pleasure.

The history of gardens is a relatively new field of research and I can do no more here than give the reader an introduction to the subject and some examples of gardens which can still be seen today. Those who wish to know more should consult the bibliography on page 160.

The use of symmetry and perspective at their grandest: ◀ dramatic changes of level, statuary and water orchestrated at the Villa d'Este, Italy, in the late sixteenth century; ▲ a subtle use of the same elements on a virtually flat site at Versailles, France, a century later.

The formal garden tradition in the modern period arose out of the desire of humanist scholars and architects of the Italian Renaissance to re-create the gardens of classical antiquity. These gardens, of course, had not survived and the designers had to rely on literary sources for guidance when reconstructing them. The architectural treatise of Vitruvius (first century BC) and the letters of Pliny the Younger (c. AD 61–112) were the most significant sources. The Italian architect Leon Battista Alberti (1404 –72) synthesized this material into the first statement on the formal garden ever made in his 'Ten Books of Architecture', *De re aedificatoria Libri X*, 1452.

Alberti described the garden for the first time in terms of geometry, as a direct extension of the house with ordered pergolas, trees planted in avenues, topiary, a wild garden, an amphitheatre, grottoes, a labyrinth and the use of water and statuary, and his influence caused the re-ordering of medieval gardens to accord with these concepts. Even more fundamental than this, Alberti applied to gardening the rules founded on harmony and proportion which were to dominate architecture for the next few centuries. Gardening as architecture became an expression of a man-centred universe, where man the microcosm was the measure of everything and in whose eyes the lines of the newly discovered science of perspective met.

No garden from this period survives intact but perhaps its essence can still be captured in the garden of the Palazzo Piccolomini in Pienza, Italy, where these principles were put into practice. The palace and its garden were designed as part of a new town by the humanist Pope, Pius II, between 1459 and 1462. The garden, a perfectly proportioned rectangular enclosure, is linked to the palace by a loggia which has a view of the landscape beyond.

In 1503 the Italian architect Bramante (1444 –1512) designed the celebrated series of terraces and flights of steps which re-ordered a hillside to link the Vatican with the papal hilltop villa, the Belvedere. This spectacular solution, which was used as a setting for Pope Julius II's collection of antique sculpture, established the formal garden style in its high Renaissance phase. As a result, such built elements became essential ingredients in garden design for the next two hundred years. The inspiration behind the great villas and gardens of this period designed by Raphael (1483–1520) and his successors was the splendour of the imperial villas of ancient Rome. For the Cardinal Giulio de Medici, Raphael designed the Villa Madama in Rome, begun in 1516, the seminal example of the interpenetration of house and garden by

Levens Hall, Cumbria.

means of courts and loggias. Raphael's pupil, Giulio Romano (c.1499–1546), took the format to Mantua where, for the Gonzaga dukes, he built the Palazzo del Tè (1525–35), a villa with a walled garden, water features and a grotto. Later Vignola (1507–73), Ammanati (1511–92) and Vasari (1511–74) elaborated the theme of courtyard spaces with a new sophistication which embraced the use of water, sculpture, loggias and a nymphaeum (an architectual grotto), complemented by abundant planting, in the Villa Giulia in Rome (begun in 1551).

Later in the century this re-ordering of house and garden was taken even further by the great Venetian architect, Andrea Palladio (1508–80), in the villas he designed along the river Brenta. His work was to be widely influential north of the Alps in the design of country houses. The most famous surviving instance of his oeuvre is the Villa Barbaro at Maser, designed in the 1560s, where, uniquely, the secret garden with its nymphaeum still exists.

It was some time before the effects of these new ideas were felt in northern Europe. The earliest instance came in France, in the château gardens of Francis I (reigned 1515–47). Elements of their influence still survive at Anet and Fontainebleau, for example, but perhaps the best overall impression can be gathered from the garden designed by Philibert de l'Orme (c.1510–70) for Henri II's mistress, Diane de Poitiers, at Chenonceau in 1551.

By that date Italian garden design had entered a new phase, one which in art-historical jargon we label Mannerist. The garden became a vehicle for allegory as recondite as that which appeared in the frescoes on the walls of the palaces and villas of the period. Designers exploited changes in level on a huge scale, deployed water as spectacle and specially commissioned sculptures to create a scheme whose intention was the glorification of the owner but which, at the same time, demanded of the visitor an ability to read and enjoy the imagery. Much depended also on the manipulation of perspective by the planting of avenues and the creation of vistas. Gardens became controlled

illusion. This phase was later imitated all over Europe, reaching England only after 1600.

We are fortunate that in Italy there are some spectacular survivals of this style, gardens which still exert their spell on the visitor. The first is the Villa Lante at Bagnaia, whose design is traditionally attributed to Vignola. Built for the Cardinal Gambara, work began on the hillside site in 1566 and the design narrates the story of the four classical ages of man, using a vocabulary of grottoes, fountains, cascades and formal parterres. Not far away, at the Villa d'Este in Tivoli, Pirro Ligorio (c.1510–83), working from 1560 to 1575, orchestrated an even grander site for the Cardinal of Ferrara, creating a geometric framework of vistas interspersed with statues, fountains and other garden structures which took the visitor on a symbolic journey, making him choose, like the mythological hero Hercules, between Virtue and Pleasure. The only surviving garden of this type north of the Alps is that created for Markus Sittikus, prince-bishop of Salzburg (1612–19) at Hellbrunn. Its bizarre grottoes and waterworks were designed to make the visitor experience both the wonder and terror of the twin powers of nature and art.

These Mannerist formal gardens were not solely complex allegorical statements. They also celebrated late Renaissance man's apparent conquest of the world of nature and, as the century ended in religious dissension, demonstrated his search for some new underlying system to re-unite a shattered universe. Such gardens are not merely decoration and delight: they are monuments to the aspirations and tensions of a culture moving out of magic and into science.

The lead in formal garden style passed in the seventeenth century from Italy to France. One man, André le Nôtre (1613–1700), and one garden, Versailles, created for the Sun King, Louis XIV, between 1665 and 1683, epitomized the change. Garden design became one of the supreme expressions of absolutism. Whereas Renaissance garden design had been about the subjection of nature to man the microcosm, Baroque garden design may be said to have been about the subjection of nature to the monarch. The lines of the garden's vistas and perspectives radiated from the palace as if from the monarch's eyes, and its many 'rooms' were open-air state apartments. Magnificence and splendour were the key notes, for Versailles and gardens like it were designed to glorify the monarch and as a setting for courtly ritual and entertainment. As a result they became even larger, subjugating the surrounding landscape by thrusting out into it avenues of trees and vistas on the major axes from the palace, and extending a rigid grid of hierarchically arranged parterres and *pièces d'eau*, enhanced by subtle changes of level to create surprise.

Le Nôtre was responsible for a long series of royal gardens in France and even sent plans to England for Greenwich Palace. His influence was felt throughout Europe. Every court emulated and adapted the French style: in England in the work of George London (d.1714) and Henry Wise (1653–1738), in the Low Countries in that of Daniel Marot (1661–1752), in Sweden in that of Nicodemus Tessin the Younger (1679–1719) and in Russia in that of Jean-Baptiste-Alexandre le Blond (1679–1719).

There is no shortage of palace gardens in the Baroque style to visit, apart from Versailles, but perhaps the two most spectacular are at Peterhof on the coast near Leningrad (Petrodvorets), designed for Peter the Great between 1716 and 1719, which boasts a famous water cascade from which golden statues arise, and the recently restored garden of William III at Het Loo, Apeldoorn, in the Netherlands, laid out by the French Hugeuenot Daniel Marot, who began work in 1686.

In the aftermath of the Napoleonic wars Het Loo was turned into an English-style landscape garden by the simple expedient of burying it beneath a substantial layer of soil (which meant that over a century later the original garden could be excavated). Hundreds of other baroque gardens across Europe were also swept away in favour of the same style.

Meanwhile in England after 1815, the reverse happened, for the formal style was rediscovered — first by Humphry Repton (1752–1818), who began designing gardens in a vaguely sixteenth- and seventeenth-century idiom for some of the country's older houses, including Beaudesert in Staffordshire (1814), but above all by John Claudius Loudon (1783–1843) who expressed his admiration for the surviving formal gardens of England in a great number of widely read books. So influential was his writing that it led to the restoration and re-creation of many of these gardens. The most famous instance of this is at Levens Hall in Cumbria, where the bones of a garden designed between 1689 and 1712 were totally re-worked by the head gardener between 1810 and 1862 to give us what we now regard as the *locus classicus* of the formal topiary gardens of Olde Englande. During the 1840s the planting of Elizabethan- and Jacobean-style formal gardens around manor houses of those periods became widespread. Hatfield House in Hertfordshire, a house built at the beginning of the seventeenth century, had appropriate gardens laid out in the

Hidcote Manor, Gloucestershire.

1840s by the second marquess (1791–1868), some of which were accepted as authentic Jacobean by the close of the century. Results like this can still deceive us today, but such gardens are a valid formal style and re-creations of this kind continue to be planted.

The nineteenth century ransacked the past for garden styles just as it did for architectural ones. The pioneer of the Italian style in England was Sir Charles Barry (1795–1860), who revived the use of terracing, gravel instead of grass, statuary, and the importance of evergreens. The garden of Trentham Hall in Staffordshire, begun in 1840, was his first major work in the Italian manner, and a whole series followed, using staircases, balustrading, urns and tazzas, fountains and loggias based on Renaissance gardens. Shrublands Park at Ipswich, in Suffolk, designed by Barry between 1851 and 1854, remains a powerful reminder of the grandeur of this style, with a huge sweeping staircase descending a hill which once led to the formal parterres spread out below. At the turn of the century interest was fuelled again, by writers such as Edith Wharton (1862–1937) and Sir George Sitwell (1860–1943), and a series of Italianate gardens were created in England, the USA, and, indeed, in Italy itself. Of these perhaps the most famous are La Pietra at Florence in Italy, created by the Englishman Arthur Acton from 1904; at Hever Castle in Kent, England, designed by Pearson and Cheal for the American, William Waldorf Astor, from 1903; and at the Villa Vizcaya in Florida, USA, designed between 1912 and 1916.

The French Baroque style was also revived in England in the 1840s by William Andrews Nesfield (1793–1881) when he began to design a long series of elaborate *parterres de broderie* in box and coloured gravels. The style had lost favour in England by the close of the century, one of its last manifestations being the *parterre d'eau* by Achille Duchêne (1866–1947) at Blenheim Palace (completed 1930). He, together with his father, Henri (1841–1902), started the restoration of the French parks and gardens in the Baroque style and created new

ones. At Courances in Essonne, France, before 1914, Achille achieved an outstanding re-creation of a traditional seventeenth-century garden layout.

In the United States the response to such revivalism was eclecticism on a vast scale, as multi-millionaires created formal gardens that included in their design the whole historic repertory. Two of the most grandiose examples are Biltmore House in North Carolina (built in the 1890s for George W. Vanderbilt) and the Hearst Gardens at San Simeon, California (begun in 1922).

As the century drew to its close, the emphasis in England shifted from outright revivalism to a search for a garden style related to rural traditions that would make use of vernacular materials and techniques. This merged with a movement which rejected the revival of foreign formal styles in favour of what was believed to be the Olde English garden. The most famous exponents of the resulting style were the architect Sir Edwin Lutyens (1869–1944) and the garden designer Gertrude Jekyll (1843–1932). Together they created seventy gardens between 1889 and 1912, and in them they expounded a new synthesis that married architectural formality using native materials for structure with a planting designed to soften rather than accentuate the geometry, making full use of the vast expansion in available plant varieties that had occurred during the nineteenth century. The garden at Hestercombe in Somerset, designed in 1903 and reinstated in 1973, remains the most accessible example of their style at its very best.

The two gardens which have exerted more influence on garden design in England in the late twentieth century than any others are also formal in structure. The first is at Hidcote Manor in Gloucestershire, designed during the course of about 30 years by an American, Lawrence Johnston (1871–1958), who acquired the house in 1907, and the second is at Sissinghurst Castle in Kent, created by Vita Sackville-West (1892–1962) and Sir Harold Nicolson between 1930 and 1962. They remain enduring testimonies to the strength of the Lutyens-Jekyll tradition in garden design and the resistance to Modernism in England as expressed in the new discipline of landscape architecture.

Between the two world wars the rejection of the Victorian age and the rediscovery of the eighteenth century led to a widespread abandonment of formality. It was the era of the island bed and the miniaturization of elements from the landscape tradition, and has resulted in some of the sadder manifestations of present-day garden design.

RE-CREATING FORMAL GARDENS

NORTHERN RENAISSANCE GARDEN

1 *Juniperus communis* 'Hibernica'
2 Santolina
3 Gravel
4 Purple stocks
5 Golden dwarf box
6 Gravel
7 Standard holly
8 Green dwarf box
9 White stocks

SEVENTEENTH-CENTURY TURF AND TOPIARY GARDEN

1 Hornbeam
2 Turf
3 Yew obelisks
4 Brick edging
5 Gravel
6 Hawthorn mopheads
7 Urn

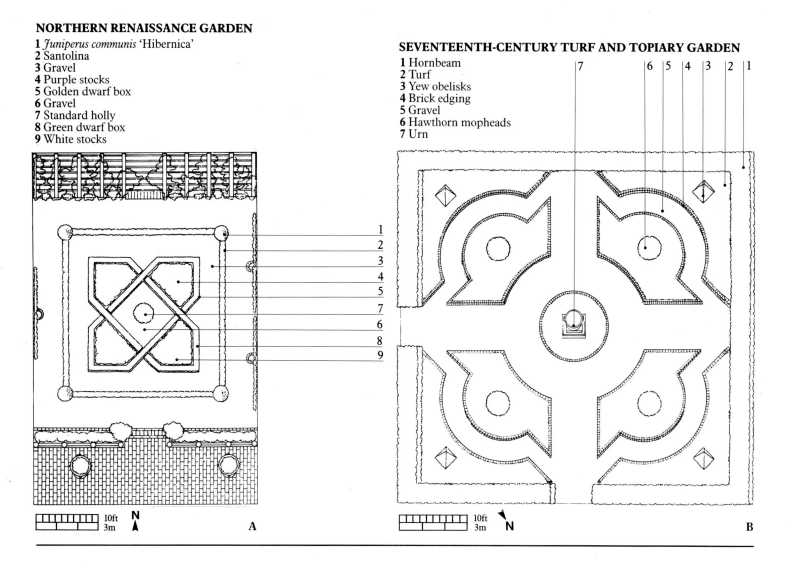

10ft
3m
N
A

10ft
3m
N
B

There is no such thing as an accurate re-creation of a garden from the past. As in the case of interior decoration or historical plays or films, elements of the designer's time always creep in, however rigorous the criteria, and where gardens are concerned, there are additional complications, especially in planting.

The problems of trying to use authentic plants have to be faced in any restoration. It is not always possible to identify which plants were grown in the gardens of a particular period and the patchiness of the visual records can make it difficult even to know what a plant looked like. Even when we have the name of a plant, its identification is not necessarily straightforward, and the problem is often acute for gardens dating from before the mid-eighteenth century when the system of plant classification devised by Linnaeus (1707–78) was published.

Furthermore, many old varieties have disappeared completely and, even among those that survive, some are difficult to obtain.

We also do not always know either how to read or how to interpret garden plans in manuscripts or in the old gardening books. A typical instance of this problem occurs in the case of knot gardens. The patterns supplied in such books as *The Countrie Housewifes Garden* (1617) are sometimes so incredibly complicated that one wonders whether they were ever planted, or if they were — and this is more to the point — how. There is no commentary as to the exact plants used, no indication of scale or discussion of maintenance. It is hardly surprising, therefore, that no two re-creations of a knot garden ever look quite the same.

We must also acknowledge that we would dislike many of the authentic ingredients of the

old formal gardens and, indeed, would find some of them positively disturbing in our own gardens. The crude use of lumps of coal for the black ground in a parterre, for instance, or the wide spacing of plants so that each one could be seen as a single specimen, would both be unnerving as visual experiences in late twentieth-century terms. The use of brilliant primary colours and abundant gilding, together with polychrome sculpture, which were considered the norm for centuries, we would find equally strange and off-key.

A serious approach to the re-creation of historic gardens began before 1914, when Ernest Law planted an Elizabethan garden at New Place, Stratford-on-Avon in Warwickshire. Between 1906 and 1924 there was an even more spectacular re-creation of a sixteenth-century French château garden at Villandry,

BAROQUE PARTERRE
1 Box **2** Gravel

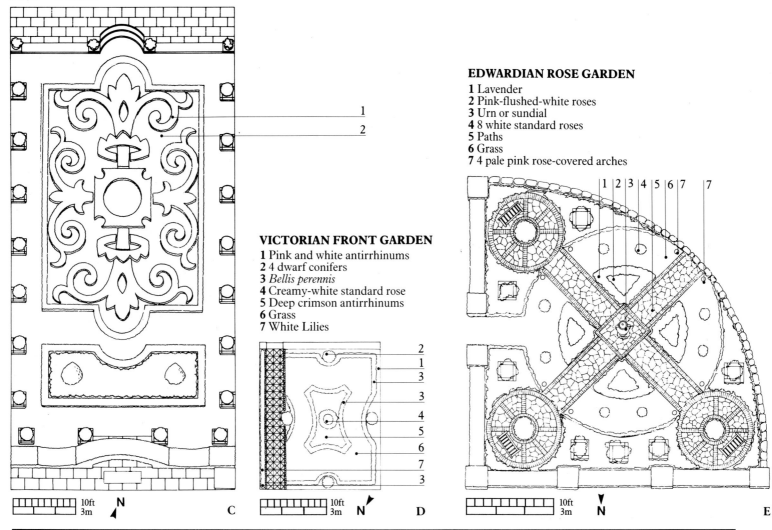

1
2

EDWARDIAN ROSE GARDEN
1 Lavender
2 Pink-flushed-white roses
3 Urn or sundial
4 8 white standard roses
5 Paths
6 Grass
7 4 pale pink rose-covered arches

1 2 3 4 5 6 7   7

VICTORIAN FRONT GARDEN
1 Pink and white antirrhinums
2 4 dwarf conifers
3 *Bellis perennis*
4 Creamy-white standard rose
5 Deep crimson antirrhinums
6 Grass
7 White Lilies

2
1
3
3
4
5
6
7
3

10ft
3m   N   C

10ft
3m   N   D

10ft
3m   N   E

Indre-et-Loire. But the real advent of garden history as a scholarly discipline dates only from the 1970s. Nevertheless it has already stimulated an intense interest in historic gardens. In England the re-creation by the National Trust of a number of seventeenth-century formal gardens for certain of their period houses has inevitably fuelled this interest. For the first time these styles can be seen, copied or adapted. Add to this the new concern with old plants, which has led to a genuine desire to preserve and record the old varieties, and the conditions for the revivalist have never been better.

In the five garden designs which follow, and of which the ground plans (*above*) are variations, I am painfully aware of the constraints and limitations of so-called re-creation; that is why I have called them 'evocations'. They can never

rise much above the level of pastiche. They are meant for gardens of today, which tend to be small, and are therefore necessarily a contradiction of styles — such as the Baroque — which demand a large scale. On the other hand, why deny ourselves the pleasure of such a style if its elements can be adapted to a small area, as I have tried to do? My intention has been to re-create the spirit of a particular type of historical formal garden in an idiom which is, I hope, acceptable today in terms of planting, maintenance and budget. Although I have designed each garden to a particular size and aspect, and any of the designs could be adapted, or enlarged or reduced in proportion, to accommodate different dimensions. The option to make any of these designs more historically correct is open but with the proviso that the result can never be more than approximate.

ALTERNATIVE EVOCATIONS
▲ These groundplans show other ways of treating the central area of the gardens that follow.
A 'The Diamond Knot'. This knot, which replaces the parterre (page 35) is based on one in Marriott's *Knots for Gardens* (1615).
B Gothic Turf Garden. This is based on one of Meager's designs in *The English Gardener* (1670), but uses curved not straight lines (page 39).
C French Parterre. This scrollwork, which dispenses with the water (page 43), is derived from elements of parterres designed by Le Nôtre.
D Bedding Garden. This is based on one of Loudon's designs in *The Gardener's Magazine* (1835). Height and a focal point are provided by a standard rose instead of an urn (page 47).
E Country Rose Garden. This is a re-working of the Jekyllesque garden (page 51), but uses four rose arches instead of the pergola.

NORTHERN RENAISSANCE GARDEN

NORTHERN RENAISSANCE GARDEN

The essence of a renaissance garden was its geometry. Earth and plants were arranged as though by a mathematician to form regular flat symmetrical patterns. I have based this design on what would have been familiar in northern Europe during the late sixteenth and early seventeenth centuries; a formula evolved as the new renaissance influences percolated north of the Alps from Italy, imposing on the medieval garden a new order as well as bringing features like grottoes, fountains and statuary.

Whether in Spain, France or England there are certain features which are common to all renaissance gardens. One is the attitude to nature as a hostile element to be shut out. The mounts and terraces in these gardens were made to enable the visitor to look down on the pattern of the garden and certainly not to look out at views beyond, except perhaps to spot a warring army approaching. Pattern is the key ingredient in the design and it comes as no surprise to learn that these could be supplied by embroiderers. The gardens were either a single or several enclosed rectangular spaces surrounded by walls with galleries or pergolas on one or more sides. Later it became the norm to surround gardens with raised terraces so as to appreciate the patterns; for the same reason they were often sited where they could be looked down upon from the main reception rooms of a house which would have been situated on the first floor.

Within its rectangular area the garden would have been subdivided into a series of identical squares or rectangles, each one surrounded by its own hedge, often with a juniper at the corner. Within each of those separate gardens the format and pattern could vary. (The evolution of the parterre is discussed on pages 54–61). There could, for example, be a maze or alternatively, raised beds held in by planks of wood in a geometric pattern. Equally, there could be knots — patterns created by interlacing ribbons of low growing hedges. Knots would be laid out in a mixture of plants — box, santolina, thyme, rosemary or germander — in intricate formal patterns requiring regular clipping. The focal point of an entire garden was usually a central fountain, but each knot or geometric compartment had its own focal point too, which could often be a single small tree or a piece of topiary carried out in holly, hawthorn, rosemary or box (yew came later).

Everywhere one senses the ruler and compasses to hand as trees, shrubs and flowers were pruned and shaped into squares and circles, cones and pyramids. The intention was to reimpose on untamed nature that perfect harmony of proportion which it had once known at God's hands before man's fall from grace.

THE EVOCATION

It is perfectly possible to re-create the spirit of these early gardens on a small scale by combining the basic elements in a design which is recognizably renaissance. It is an ideal solution for a small town or walled cottage garden. Enclosure is essential, whether by walls, hedges or pergolas. Depending on the space available the garden should be laid out in one or more squares or rectangles of exactly the same size. Within those the pattern can vary. The illustration (*right*) shows a symmetrical arrangement of beds outlined in box hedging, and on page 30 there is an alternative option — for a typical yet easily maintained knot.

This elementary geometric lay-out of beds is typical of the late sixteenth and early seventeenth centuries and was used indiscriminately for gardens of turf, of raised beds or beds defined by low hedges; in any of these forms it was known as a parterre. The overall combination of pergola, parterre and balustrading owes much to a famous print which depicts a Dutch garden in Crispin van de Passe's *Hortus Floridus* (1615).

The simple geometric pattern for the central parterre is derived from one for a turf garden in an engraving in Salomon de Caus's work on hydraulics, *Les Raisons des Forces Mouvantes* (1615). De Caus (*c.* 1576-1626) was a French Huguenot who had visited Italy in the 1590s and seen the famous mannerist gardens with their spectacular effects. He transported these ideas north of the Alps when he worked in Flanders, England, and Germany where he created the legendary *Hortus Palatinus* in Heidelberg.

If you are ambitious you may wish to attempt one of the complex patterns which are often reproduced in books on the history of gardening. They require contrasting planting (for instance of two different colours of dwarf box, or box and santolina) to emphasize the interlacing. When you clip, you must remember to observe the changes in height where the varieties interweave.

The pergola at the far end is of a type which goes back to the Middle Ages, but was constructed like this from the late sixteenth to the close of the seventeenth century, and appears in this form in countless contemporary paintings and engravings. It would have surrounded one or more sides of the garden area. Reconstructed examples can be seen at Ham House, Surrey, England, and at the palace of Het Loo, Apeldoorn, the Netherlands, where hornbeam has been trained over it. The simple wooden balustrading which I have put along the terrace next to the house appears in the same sources.

This garden has been designed for a site that is totally enclosed by walls, which would allow a typical period planting of espaliered fruit trees, two apples (**1** and **2**) on a south- or west-facing wall and a fan-trained cherry (**3**). Specialist nurseries do carry historic fruit trees but you are unlikely to get any apples dating from much before the late seventeenth century. The pergola here (**4**) is quite an elaborate construction and calls for a qualified carpenter. It would be perfectly possible to improvise a simpler one, but avoid larch poles which will look Victorian. It should be painted the same colour as the wooden balustrading (**5**) at the terrace end. At the time the wood would have been gilded and painted and marbled in quite strong primary colours in a way we would find disturbing. It would be safer, therefore, to stick to shades of blue-green or the off-whites and greys, with a preference for the former to add an illusion of depth to the garden. Beneath the central arch there is a simple wooden seat (**6**); and there are windows either side, but room enough within perhaps to conceal a small toolshed. The pergola anyway will be concealed in time by plants which could include honeysuckle, hornbeam, jasmine, ivy, clematis, vines and eglantine.

The garden's focal point is the central parterre, with tiny gravel paths between the beds and a gravel path around it. The beds are edged with dwarf box (*Buxus sempervirens* 'Suffructicosa') with topiary box cones (**7**) at the corners and a standard sweet bay (**8**) at the centre to add height. In an authentic period planting of these beds each flower would be spaced apart in order to be looked at as a single specimen. There would be no block planting but a scattering of various spring and summer flowers of varieties available at the time. From a modern viewpoint, however, the effect of block planting will be more striking and certainly easier to cope with in terms of ground cover to suppress weeds. The illustration shows the garden in spring with white hyacinths in the centre bed (**9**), streaked Rembrandt tulips in the four spandrels (**10**), and an underplanting of old varieties and species of narcissus and snake's head fritillaries in the corner beds (**11**). Few of these varieties will be completely authentic — the hyacinths have too many pips and the Rembrandt tulips, although resembling those in the old paintings, are a post-1889 cultivar — but they are a reasonable approximation. In the summer I would plant the centre and corner beds with calendulas in shades of orange and yellow and the spandrels with the lovely single blue *Campanula persicifolia*. The garden is approached from a brick terrace (**12**) flanked by two narrow beds (**13**), filled with herbs:

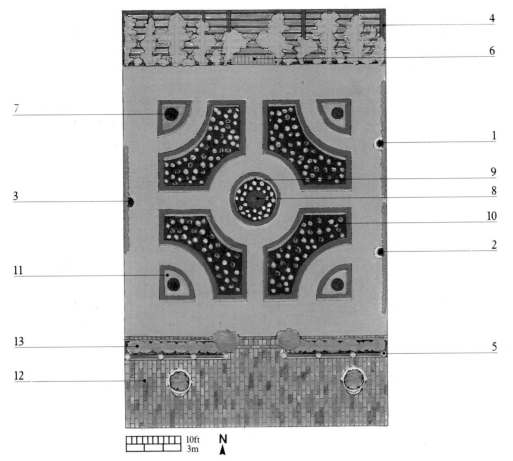

7

3

11

13

12

4

6

1

9

8

10

2

5

10ft
3m

N

rosemary, rue, thyme and sage. It is important that the terrace is raised at least slightly so one can look down on the parterre or knot. Renaissance gardens were full of plants in pots containing, for example, crown imperials in the spring, followed by carnations and *Lilium candidum* in the summer.

RENAISSANCE PLANTS

During the sixteenth century a great many new plants arrived from Turkey, Persia and the New World, greatly expanding the limited repertory available to the medieval gardener. The sixteenth century also saw the foundation of botanic gardens, such as those at the universities of Padua (1545) and Leiden (1587). It was an age of avid plant collectors like Charles L'Ecluse (1526–1609) and John Tradescant (d.1638) whose names live on today in certain plant varieties. All of this occurred at the same time that the art of painting began to explore the natural world with minute exactitude — as exemplified by Dürer's famous botanical studies. The botanical illustrator as an artist in his own right emerged in figures such as Giacomo Ligozzi (c. 1547–1626) and Jacques Le Moyne des Morgues (c. 1533–88). And, for the first time, the new art of engraving

contributed to the earliest illustrated dictionaries of plants, famous publications such as John Gerard's *The Herball* (1597), which are the sources which enables us to know so much about Renaissance plants. In spite of this, however, it is often difficult to be certain about what plants were grown at this early period; we can do little more today than look for modern varieties which approximate as closely as possible to the ones pictured in those sources. Gardeners who wish to be as exact as possible will need to consider this carefully but most of us will be content to plant in the spirit of the period.

Roses *Rosa alba, R. gallica, R. gallica* var. *officinalis, R. canina* (dog rose), *R. rubiginosa* (Eglantine), *R. damascena* 'Versicolor' (York and Lancaster), *R. foetida, R. foetida* 'Bicolor'.
Climbers *Hedera* (ivy), *Jasminum officinale* (jasmine), *Lonicera* (honeysuckle), *Clematis flammula, C. cirrhosa, C. viticella, Humulus lupulus* (hop), *Vitis vinifera* (grapevine).
Shrubs *Daphne mezereum, Buxus sempervirens* (box), *Berberis vulgaris, Viburnum opulus* (guelder rose), *Cornus mas, Lavandula angustifolia, L. stoechas, Ligustrum vulgare* (not *L. ovalifolium*), *Prunus laurocerasus* (common laurel), *Santolina chamaecyparissus, Cytisus*

scoparius (common broom).
Herbs *Filipendula ulmaria* (meadowsweet), *Hyssopus* (hyssop), *Rosmarinus* (rosemary), *Ruta graveolens* (rue), *Salvia officinalis* (sage), *S. solarea, S. viridis, Saponaria officinalis* (soapwort), *Tanacetum vulgare* (tansy), *Thymus serpyllum* (thyme), *T. vulgaris, Foeniculum vulgare* (fennel), *Origanum majorana* (majoram).
Perennials *Achillea ptarmica, A. millefolium, Althaea* (hollyhock), *Aconitum napellus, A. septentrionale, Adonis, Aquilegia vulgaris, Armeria, Artemisia abrotanum, A. absinthium, A. vulgaris, Astrantia major, Bellis perennis, Campanula glomerata, C. latifolia, C. persicifolia, Dianthus caryophyllus* (carnation), *D. plumarius* (pinks), *Gentiana verna, Geranium pratense* (meadow cranesbill), *G. sanguineum* (bloody cranesbill), *Geum urbanum, G. rivale, Helleborus niger, H. foetidus, H. viridis, Hemerocallis flava* (day lily), *H. fulva, Hepatica, Iris foetida, I. pallida, Nepeta cataria* (catmint), *Paeonia officinalis, Polygonatum* (Solomon's seal), *Primula vulgaris* (primrose), *P. auricula, P. veris* (cowslip), *Ranunculus asiaticus, Tradescantia virginiana, Verbascum* (mullein), *Vinca minor, V. major, Viola odorata* (violet), *V. tricolor* (pansy).
Annuals *Amaranthus caudatus, A. gangeticus, Antirrhinum, Calendula officinalis* (marigold), *Chrysanthemum segetum* (corn marigold), *Delphinium consolida* (larkspur), *Iberis umbellata* (candytuft), *Papaver somniferum* (opium poppy), *P. rhoeas* (field poppy).
Hardy annuals *Althaea* (hollyhock), *Helianthus annuus* (annual sunflower), *Lychnis chalcedonica, Nigella damascena* (love-in-a-mist), *Scabiosa, Tagetes erecta* (African marigolds), *T. patula* (French marigold).
Hardy biennials *Cheiranthus* (wallflower), *Dianthus barbatus* (sweet William), *Digitalis* (foxglove), *Lunaria annua* (honesty), *Matthiola incana* (stock or gillyflower).
Bulbous plants *Allium moly, Anemone coronaria, A. × fulgens, A. nemorosa, Convallaria* (lily-of-the-valley), *Crocus susianus, Cyclamen persicum, Erythronium dens-canis* (dog's-tooth-violet), *Fritillaria imperialis* (crown imperial), *F. meleagris* (snake's head), *F. persica, Hyacinthus, Leucojum aestivum* (snowflake), *L. autumnale, L. vernum, Lilium candidum, L. martagon, Narcissus pseudonarcissus* (lent lily), *N. hispanicus, N. poeticus, N. jonquilla, N. triandrus, Ornithogalum umbellatum* (star of Bethlehem), *Scilla, Tulipa*.
Plants used in pots *Lilium candidum, Chrysanthemum frutescens* (marguerite), *Dianthus caryophyllus* (carnation).

17TH CENTURY
TURF AND TOPIARY
GARDEN

SEVENTEENTH-CENTURY TURF AND TOPIARY GARDEN

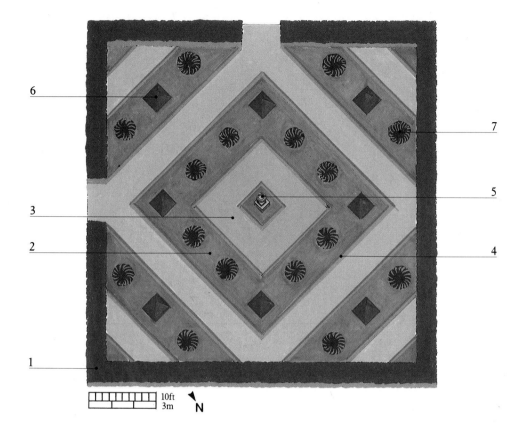

One of the most familiar types of formal garden in the sixteenth and seventeenth centuries was the turf garden which was essentially a parterre, a pattern created out of grass and gravel. As time moved on, the designs became more complex as they reflected the developing characteristics of the Mannerist or Baroque movements in the arts.

Our approach to the use of grass today is largely inherited from the landscape tradition which called for rich irregular swathes of verdant green as a setting for a naturalistic planting of trees and shrubs. But we have also inherited the way in which its formal use was revived in the Victorian age when the cult of the perfect lawn, as the surface into which geometric beds were cut, provided the classic foil for foliage and flowers. In Renaissance and Baroque gardens, however, grass was a much-prized garden feature in itself. In an age before machinery it had high maintenance implications and was often the prime ingredient of a garden composition, used in the centre and not pushed to the periphery. In fact gravel was used where we now tend to use grass.

The medieval pleasure garden in one of its forms — the 'herber' — consisted mostly of lawn intersected by paths with a fountain in the centre. The Renaissance inherited this delight in cultivated and cut grass and developed it into a whole branch of garden art known as *gazon coupé*, literally 'cut turf'. The turf was cut into geometric patterns, often of great intricacy, and the areas between filled with coloured earths, sand or gravel. Within the turf itself the formal pattern would be emphasized by a symmetrical planting of trees and shrubs or topiary.

The earliest extensive collection of designs for turf gardens appears in a book by the Dutch artist, Hans Vredeman de Vries. (1527–1606) *Hortorum viridariorumque elegantes et multiplices formae* (1583). His designs, which were to be pan-European in their influence, were enormously elaborate in the fantastic style of northern Mannerism, yet always set within a rectilinear frame and always placed within an enclosure formed by wooden architecture and pergolas.

The principles of these very early turf gardens were carried over into the seventeenth century when the bizarre Mannerist patterns were replaced by the bolder curved forms of the Baroque. In that era they became known as *parterres à l'anglaise*, in deference both to the quality of English greensward and to the English predilection for grass *plats*, plain geometric shapes, with fountains and statues placed within them as against the elaborate parterre forms more favoured on the continent. André Mollet (d. *c*.1665), the French garden

designer who worked in England, includes designs for what he calls *compartiments de gazon* in his highly influential book, *Le Jardin de Plaisir* (1651). These were geometric patterns in grass and gravel surrounded by borders of flowers, a band of white sand and finally an enclosing box hedge.

Other European designers followed him with variants but in England there continued throughout the century a preference for the much simpler form, in which the flowerbeds were dispensed with and the parterre confined to cut turf patterns with a statue at the centre, the whole surrounded by a containing narrow bed which could be planted with small fruit trees, spruce, firs, topiary in the form of obelisks and standards or even dotted with container shrubs and trees in the summer.

I know of no existing accurate re-creation of a turf garden, and the only example of a re-creation of the English form of cut-work is at Little Moreton Hall in Cheshire which was re-planted in 1975. It was based on a design by Leonard Meager in his *The English Gardener* (1670). It is unfortunate that the re-creation is inaccurate, and there is grass where the gravel should be and vice versa. None the less it gives some impression of the delightful possibilities of reviving this type of garden.

THE EVOCATION
This turf garden is adapted from one in a view of Denham Place, Buckinghamshire, England, now in the Yale Center for British Art, New Haven, USA. The house was built between 1688 and 1701 by Sir Roger Hill and the picture records the gardens *c*.1705. They were extensive and included parterres, an orchard, a wilderness and a long canal with a pavilion astride it in the latest Dutch manner of William and Mary. In the painting the turf garden is a rectangle with what seems to be a sundial in the central diamond with five lozenge-shaped bands of turf alternating with equal-sized bands of gravel, and with topiary in various shapes planted within the turf.

I have taken the elements of this garden and designed one which might perhaps form one room in a larger garden, for in twentieth-century terms (but not in seventeenth-century ones) it would be considered eccentric if this was to be your only garden. With its strong architectural and sculptural quality this garden would really come into its own in autumn and winter. For the hedge which encloses the area (**1**), I would suggest hornbeam (*Carpinus betulus*) as the most authentic planting. Beech (*Fagus sylvaticus*) would produce a similar effect but would not be correct for the period. The hedge is cut straight at a height of 6 feet (1.75 metres) to allow the dark green obelisk tips to peep tantalizingly over the top of it. The rusty caramel colour of the hedge in winter will also form a splendid backdrop for the dark green yew topiary to be set off to advantage. By placing a hedge around the turf garden I have created what at the time would have been called a *cabinet*. This is because I see this as a 'room' some distance from the house planted as a surprise; but if you decide to plant your turf garden near the house, dispense with the hedge and enjoy looking down on its pattern from the upstairs windows.

Within, it is divided into a series of square bands alternating turf (**2**) and gravel (**3**) but with the former held in place by brick edging sunken clear enough to allow the use of the mower (**4**). As a focal point, although a finial or statue would be more authentic, the classical urn (**5**) I have suggested could allow for some trailing ivy and perhaps a few pansies in winter, and for two further seasonal plantings. This would be inaccurate in terms of the period but a compromise that may work to bring colour into a small garden. On the bands of turf I have alternated obelisks of yew (**6**) with standards of common hawthorn (*Crataegus*) (**7**). The yew will require annual clipping and from 18-inch (40-centimetre) plants will mature into 7-foot (2-metre) specimens in about eight years if fed regularly. The hawthorn is much quicker to mature but will require more than one cutting in a season, with a sure eye needed for the globular form. Their spidery branches in winter make an intriguing contrast to both the dense velvet pile of the yew and the crinkled caramel of the hornbeam. An alternative would be to plant crab apples (decorative *Malus*), keeping them pruned to mopheads, but in the centre lozenge you would only have room for half as many as the number of standard hawthorns.

Parterres à l'anglaise were, of course, open to every geometric shape. In the seventeenth century they could be enormously elaborate with swirling Baroque patterns, impossible to maintain today without professional help. If you decide to make use of elementary curves, you will need to insert firm plastic edging to the turf to maintain the geometry.

You can choose your own planting from the list below, remembering always to keep the scheme absolutely symmetrical, to prune your trees and shrubs into shape, and to preserve a balance between evergreen and deciduous plants. You may also wish to emphasize your design by enclosing the pattern with a low box hedge, although that will, of course, present mowing problems.

Those who are really adventurous might like to consider reviving this lost garden form using twentieth-century patterns. It may be difficult to preserve symmetry but paintings by Op artists of the 1960s would provide a useful quarry for ideas for pattern.

TREES AND SHRUBS FOR HEDGES AND TOPIARY

Most of our notions of seventeenth-century topiary are derived from either nineteenth-century re-creations or overgrown and re-cut surviving gardens. There is also the poet Alexander Pope's famous denunciation of its excesses in which he lists a whole range of outlandish figures which could never actually have existed. Any study of the vast numbers of paintings and engravings of topiary of this period show that gardens depended on the mass use of a number of very simple geometric shapes either planted in repetition or alternately. The cone, the obelisk, the standard and the 'cake-stand' re-occur again and again. In planting a *parterre à l'anglaise* on this tiny scale do not include more than two of these basic shapes or the result will be more akin to a romantic Victorian idea of a seventeenth-century garden than the real thing.

David Jacques and Arend Jan van der Horst in their *The Gardens of William and Mary* (1988) provide an invaluable analysis of trees and shrubs as listed in the six major English and Dutch gardening publications which appeared between John Evelyn's *Sylva, or a Discourse of Forest Trees* (1664) and Stephen Switzer's *Ichnographia Rustica* (1718). The nine most popular plants for hedges and topiary are listed below. (For further horticultural information on these, see pages 148-50.)

Buxus sempervirens (common box)
There are many varieties of box but all retain its most typical feature, shiny compact dense green leaves. The most vigorous form for larger topiary is 'Handsworthensis' which has very dark green leaves. The variegated forms are less vigorous but really gorgeous with leaves edged with silver ('Elegantissima'), or splashed ('Aureovariegata') or tipped ('Gold Tip') with gold. Well-placed combinations of the two can produce a stunning effect. The same gold marking can be had in the dwarf version 'Suffruticosa' which is used for edging and knots.

Carpinus betulus (hornbeam)
This, like beech, retains its leaves through the winter providing a dramatic russet foil to evergreens. If you use it for a stilt hedge or a palisade the trunk is attractive in itself, starting grey and later, with age, becoming fluted.

Crataegus monogyna (common hawthorn)
Common hawthorn makes a fast hedge with white flowers in spring and haws in the autumn. It was already used for topiary in the sixteenth century and can be clipped easily into simple geometric shapes such as obelisks or standards. It is useful for the striking contrast it makes to the denser evergreens in winter; as it is deciduous, it sheds its leaves to reveal an intriguing spidery twiggy form.

Ilex aquifolium (common English holly)
Holly requires enormous patience but it is of such beauty that it is worth waiting for. The effect of light on its spiky dark green leaves give a unique surface refraction which is more lively than any of the other evergreens. There is a large number of different cultivars available today which make ideal subjects for topiary because of the colouring of their leaves: for example, 'Aureomarginata' and 'Golden King' are margined with a clear yellow; those of 'Silver Queen' and 'Handsworth New Silver' are margined and sometimes splashed with white.

Juniperus communis (common juniper)
Junipers were used in the seventeenth century as upright sentinels at the corners of parterres. They were the nearest approximation in northern Europe that could be had to the Italian cypress. *J. c.* 'Hibernica' is blue-grey in tone and of slender and elegant form. It was only when many of the junipers were killed by the very severe winters which were such a feature of the last decades of the century that the indestructible yew was generally adopted.

Ligustrum vulgare (privet)
Not to be confused with the modern *L. ovalifolium*, its growth rate is fast and it can be used for both hedges and topiary but will require clipping more than once in a season.

Phillyrea angustifolia
Much used in Stuart times, but rarely in our own, and now not easily available. Being very dense in reponse to regular clipping it can be used for hedges and topiary. Its elongated shiny leaves are a dark green.

Pyracantha coccinea (firethorn)
A hardy evergreen shrub whose thorny branches bear white flowers in the early summer and brilliant orange berries in the autumn. This is suitable for hedging up to 6 feet (2 metres) but will climb higher when grown against a wall.

Rhamnus alaternus (Italian buckthorn)
A large easily grown bushy evergreen shrub with shiny dark green leaves and pale green flowers in spring followed by black fruits. It was used in the seventeenth century for hedging. There is a silver dappled form 'Argenteovariegata'.

BAROQUE PARTERRE

BAROQUE PARTERRE

The Baroque parterre was one of the supreme expressions of French garden art which, under the aegis of Le Nôtre, dominated European garden design for over a century. As an element of garden design it emerged in France in the 1620s and 1630s but it was the result of a long evolution which had its roots in Italy more than a century and a half earlier. Yet the very fact that we still use the word parterre demonstrates that whatever its origins the parterre remains French in character.

What might be described as the earliest designs for parterres appeared in a book by Francesco Colonna entitled the *Hypnerotamachia Polyphili*, published in Venice in 1499. The practice of laying out gardens in figured patterns goes back to antiquity but Colonna was the first writer to provide details and designs and, as the book was translated into virtually every major European language during the sixteenth century, it came to have a profound influence. Although it is, in fact, a romance, the woodcut illustrations include topiary designs and flowerbed groundplans with details of the planting.

The earliest manifestation of the influence of this work in France was in Diane de Poitiers' garden at the Château d'Anet, begun in 1546 — the same year in which the book was translated into French. There were twenty-four rectangular beds, known as 'compartiments'. They were planted with flowers and herbs in complex patterns, including some laid out with an 'H' for Henri II (Diane was his mistress), and others with a crescent moon in tribute to Diane as goddess of the chase. These beds were sited close to the terrace so that their symbolic content could be readily studied. They needed major maintenance and frequent re-planting to retain their intricate patterns. During the second half of the century there followed a steady stream of books with designs for similar *compartiments*, the most influential series were included in Charles Etienne and Jean Liébault's *L'Agriculture et Maison Rustique* which first appeared in 1564.

The great step forward in the development of the parterre was taken by Claude Mollet, gardener to Henri IV, in the early 1580s under the instruction of Etienne du Perac, architect to the Duc d'Aumâle, who had inherited Anet. At Anet, Mollet planted the first *parterre de broderie*, which essentially drew together all the *compartiments* into a single repeating overall pattern. He also eventually came to use box in preference to other hedging plants, as it withstood the rigours of the northern climate. In 1595 he laid out the first *parterre de broderie* for Henri IV at Fontainebleau. Mollet's style

was hesitant, his designs literally repeated the same pattern in the four quarters but in doing so brought a new unity into garden composition.

It was to be his children, also gardeners of distinction, who developed the form away from his stiff angularity into the flowing lacy patterns that anticipated the sturdier, more emphatic rhythms of the baroque. The earliest example of this lacy style was the great parterre designed for the French Queen Marie de Medici at the Luxembourg Palace, and laid out by Jacques Boyceau who began work in 1612. He later published these designs in his *Traité du Jardinage* (1638). This parterre was sited beneath the windows of the first-floor state apartments and surrounded on the other three sides by a raised terrace with walks from which to look down on the stupendous design. This was the form of parterre that was inherited by Le Nôtre. He was to develop it still further, into the form that we have come to recognize as quintessentially Baroque, in his grandest compositions for Louis XIV at Fontainebleau, Versailles and Meudon.

This development of the parterre went hand-in-hand with a new enthusiasm for using water in garden design. Treated in a specific way in France, one form of water garden came to be known as the *parterre d'eau*. It was a scheme whereby a surface of water was divided into a series of geometrical compartments. Again, this was Italian in origin; and one of the best-known examples of elaborate design using water is at the Villa Lante at Bagnaia. Here a fountain is the focus of a composition of symmetrically arranged geometric ponds which make full use of the reflective quality of water. And it was this use of flat sheets of water reflecting the sky which became such a feature of French Baroque garden style, exemplified, for instance, at Versailles with its *parterre d'eau*, huge articulating canals and circular pools of water interrupted only by a solitary central jet.

But perhaps the major development in garden design of the seventeenth century was the vast increase in the scale and scope of the projects. As in the previous century garden sites remained basically flat, articulated only by slight changes of level, apart from the grand descent from palace or house via the terrace. But seventeenth-century gardens were huge; they dominated their surroundings by penetrating the landscape with avenues of trees radiating out from the palace or house. The whole garden scheme was conceived as a celebration of the submission of nature to man and, in particular, to the monarch. It was a style which lost its meaning with the collapse of absolutism in Europe from 1789.

THE EVOCATION

It is not easy to shrink into a tiny area the principal elements of a Baroque garden whose essence was grandeur of scale. Here, however, we have a modest scheme which brings together some of the major ingredients in a way which might be appropriate for a small urban garden, or for an enclosed area close to the house in a country garden. It is important to be able to look down upon its dominating feature, a box parterre flanking a long rectangle of water whose mirror-like qualities are only disturbed by a single central jet.

A garden in the Baroque idiom is not a cheap project and this would be by far the most expensive of our five historical evocations. The terrace (**1**) needs to be of stone or reconstituted stone, as indeed must be the balustrading (**2**) whose piers might bear urns (**3**) for seasonal plantings. This is a garden scheme which ideally calls for a surrounding wall (**4**), whitewashed, across which treillage and arcading (**5**) might run, the arches framing Versailles tubs containing topiary in box or bay (**6**). (The Versailles tub owes its name to the palace garden which was full of them placed in symmetrical arrangements to emphasize the patterns of the parterre. In that period they would have contained hothouse exotics or lemon or orange trees which were kept under cover in winter and transported out for the summer months. This is, of course, an extravagant option which is open to you.) The treillage should be painted blue-green, as it is in the re-created Baroque garden at Het Loo. The surrounding paths (**7**) are all gravelled. The pool (**8**), which need only be shallow, would be a major capital outlay, the basin requiring a retaining wall (**9**) in materials matching the terrace and steps (**10**).

Either side of the sheet of water, dwarf box is planted in a mirror image in a bold scroll pattern typical of the Baroque era (**11**), the whole being held in and defined by a containing rectangular hedge (**12**).

The scroll design I have based loosely on one for a parterre in *The Retir'd Gardener* which the two owners of the famous Brompton nurseries, George London and Henry Wise, translated from two French works, *Le jardinier solitaire* (1704) by François Gentil (dates unknown) and *Le jardinier fleuriste et historiographe* by Louis Liger (1658–1717). This gives eleven designs for parterres of different kinds.

Box parterres were frequently surrounded by a band about 4 feet (1 metre) in width, edged on either side with box, in which flowers were planted like botanical specimens 3–4 feet (about 1 metre) apart and punctuated by a symmetrical

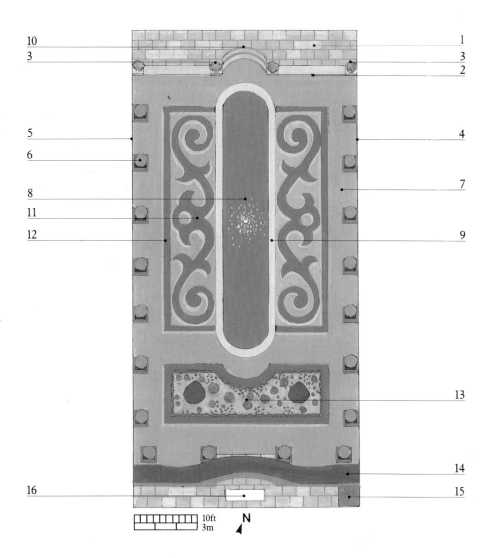

10
3

1
3
2

5
6

4

8
11
12

7

9

13

14
16

15

10ft
3m

N

Plantes (the plates alone published in 1701). By 1700 the list of plants and their cultivars was extensive and only a small selection can be given here.

PLANT SELECTION

A reasonably authentic garden could be planted using the following plants together with those listed on page 35. Modern plant breeding has produced, particularly in the case of annuals, varieties that are very different to those grown in the seventeenth and eighteenth centuries, so that in many instances we can only seek for approximations.

Annuals *Campanula medium* (Canterbury bells), *Celosia argentea* 'Cristata' (cockscomb), *Centaurea moschata* (sweet sultan), *Convovulus tricolor, Datura metel, Dimorphotheca annua, Echium plantagineum, Euphorbia heterophylla* (fire on the mountain), *Glaucium corniculatum* (horned poppy), *Gomphrena globosa* (globe amaranth), *Hedysarum coronarium, Helianthus annuus* (sunflower), *Ipomoea purpurea* (morning glory), *Lathyrus odoratus* (original sweet pea), *Lavatera trimestris* (mallow), *Limonium sinuatum* (sea lavender), *Lunaria annua* (honesty), *Mirabilis jalapa* (marvel of Peru), *Moluccella laevis* (bells of Ireland), *Myosotis scorpioides* (water forget-me-not), *Nicotiana tabacum* (tobacco plant), *Tropaeolum majus* (nasturtium).

Herbaceous perennials *Acanthus mollis* (bear's breeches), *Asphodeline lutea, Campanula pyramidalis* (chimney bellflower), *C. rapunculoides, Centaurea montana* (mountain knapweed), *Centranthus ruber* (red valerian), *Chrysanthemum leucanthemum* (oxeye daisy), *Dictamnus albus* (burning bush), *Digitalis lutea, Gentiana asclepiadea* (willow gentian), *Geranium phaeum* (mourning widow), *Iris florentina. I. germanica* (purple flag), *I. sibirica, Kniphofia uvaria* (red-hot poker), *Lathyrus latifolius* (perennial pea), *Lychnis chalcedonica* (campion), *Malva moschata* (musk mallow), *Monarda didyma* (Oswego tea, bee balm), *Ranunculus aconitifolius* (fair maids of France), *Trollius europaeus* (globe flower).

Bulbous plants *Corydalis solida, Muscari botryoides* (grape hyacinth), *Narcissus tazetta* (bunch-flowered narcissus), *N. triandrus albus* (angel's tears), *Tulipa clusiana* (lady tulip).

Climbers *Jasminum officinale* (common white jasmine), *Passiflora caerulea* (passion flower).

Shrubs *Arbutus unedo* (strawberry tree), *Hibiscus syriacus, Laurus nobilis* (sweet bay), *Myrtus communis* (myrtle), *Prunus lusitanica* (Portugal laurel), *Rosa centifolia* (cabbage rose), *Viburnum opulus* (guelder rose), *V. tinus* (laurustinus), *Yucca filamentosa* (palm lily).

arrangement of yew cones or obelisks. To provide some blossom and colour, I have introduced a minute version of this (**13**) and it is your decision whether to plant it in the authentic period manner or merely use it for a medley of plants as close to the ones available at the time as you can find. At the far end there is a simple arcade of yew clipped into a Baroque curve (**14**), free-standing against a wall on which there is treillage. With careful planning there might be room for a small toolstore (**15**) behind this. A seat (**16**) gives a view down the length of the garden.

If you decide to re-create a seventeenth century garden you must accept that its tonality will be shades of green and that its floral content will be minimal. Contentment comes from its perfect geometry and pattern which holds its interest all the year round.

FLOWERS IN THE SEVENTEENTH CENTURY

We know much more about flowers in the seventeenth century than in earlier periods. In the first instance there are the marvellous flower paintings of the Dutch and Flemish schools, which are a mine of information for anyone in the quest for plants which would look right in a period garden. This gives us the first evidence that we have of a genuine fascination for flowers and a keen appreciation of their decorative properties. This is reflected in the fashion for both manuscript and printed florilegia, publications issued in both the Low Countries and France, which record in detail the flowers grown. The French kings in particular patronized a long series of botanical works from Pierre Vallet's *Le Jardin du très Chrestien Henry IV* (1608) to Nicholas Robert's *Recueil des*

VICTORIAN
FRONT GARDEN

VICTORIAN FRONT GARDEN

The Victorian front garden is a recent phenomenon which England has exported all over the world. In the aftermath of the Industrial Revolution country people drifted to the town in search of work, as clerks in offices, as workers in factories and as servants to the new middle classes; and they all had to be housed. This was to be the age of suburbia, of huge developments in the way of semi-detached and terrace houses stretching seemingly to infinity, each with its own front and back garden. It was an era too of increasing prosperity, allied to a belief in intellectual and social improvement. For the first time gardening ceased to be the prerogative of the aristocratic, gentry and professional classes and spread out to embrace a large new middle-class audience. It was an enormous market, hungry for information and direction in terms of design, planting and maintenance. Its needs were to be met above all by one man, John Claudius Loudon.

Loudon wrote approximately sixty million words on the subject of gardening over forty years, in what were universally regarded as standard reference books. He also published his own journal, *The Gardener's Magazine*, which appeared from 1826 onwards. Although he began, essentially as a disciple of Uvedale Price (1747–1829), as a late and extreme exponent of the picturesque phase of the landscape style, Loudon was in fact largely responsible for the revival of interest in the formal garden. In the aftermath of the Napoleonic wars he toured Europe and was much struck by the geometric gardens he saw. In his influential *Encyclopaedia of Gardening* (1822) he wrote of the formal style: 'To say that landscape gardening is an improvement on geometric gardening is a similar misapplication of language as to say that a lawn is an improvement on a cornfield, because it is substituted in its place. It is absurd, therefore, to despise the ancient style . . .' Loudon's admiration for the surviving formal gardens of England and Europe paved the way for the full flood of renewed interest in formality in the historicist phase of the 1840s.

What is interesting, however, is that this revival coincided with the huge expansion of the urban middle classes, for the geometric style was ideally suited for adaptation to the small rectangular sites which made up their front and back gardens. Loudon's *The Suburban Gardener* (1838) is the first book which actually tells these aspiring new city gardeners what to do, codifying treatments for houses whose frontages were as little as 12–14 feet (4 metres) in width. By the 1850s the dominant style was the 'geometric gardenesque' which provided front gardens with a formal arrangement of flowerbeds in grass with gravel paths and a straight tile path up to the front door.

The front garden was a monument to public standing and show, as it often still is today. Any ornament such as a statue or an urn was regarded as a status symbol. The planting of an exotic tree, such as a monkey puzzle, as a focus betokened the same. The smallest amount of grass indicated that its owner possessed a lawn mower, an invention of the 1820s. Previously grass had been scythed but, by the 1860s, machines which could be operated by one person were mass-produced, which made these tiny lawns possible to maintain. The emphasis on flowerbeds, which had not been typical of the previous century, likewise signalled the material prosperity of the occupiers, as every summer they crammed their gardens with annuals, vibrant with hectic colour, laid out in the new bedding style.

Until then, the same flowers would never have been block planted. To have done so would have offended aesthetic sensibilities and reduced what were regarded as botanical specimens to the level of wallpaper. Bedding emerged in the 1830s and rapidly became the norm. It was made possible by new introductions and new hybrids, and was fed by the expansion in the nursery trade which, thanks to heated greenhouses, was capable of producing untold numbers of annuals ready for planting out early in June. The new style coincided with a passion for strong colour of a kind that we see reflected, for example, in pre-Raphaelite paintings, and which still survives today in municipal bedding schemes. The suburban front garden ablaze with blocks of colour looked, and was, a symbol of wealth. Its flowerbeds, like its newfangled lawn, also owed a debt to another novelty, mains water and the invention of the garden hosepipe.

Although a planting of spring bulbs was possible, the Victorian front garden, apart from its few permanent features, was a manifestation of the summer months only. It consisted of geometrically cut beds, edged and planted — usually in patterns — with newly introduced, brilliantly coloured annuals.

By the end of the century, when gardening responded to the cult of the Olde English garden and the Arts and Crafts Movement, borders could be herbaceous with delphiniums, phlox and hollyhocks infilled annually with sweet peas, stocks, asters and mignonette, with roses and honeysuckle coaxed around the front door. In this way the front garden remains one of the neglected triumphs of the Victorian age. Almost a century later, no one has yet devised a formula to replace it.

THE EVOCATION

Evoking a Victorian formal front garden is not a complex or expensive project. In the suburbs of the great Victorian cities of England — London, Newcastle, Manchester, Birmingham and Liverpool — and elsewhere, particularly in Commonwealth countries, they still exist; or rather their bones do. Often their basic structural ingredients are still there, waiting to be brought to life again. The size of such gardens is not large: for the majority of terrace and semi-detached houses, it is sometimes as little as 10 feet (3 metres) to the front door, rarely more than 30 (10). The garden is almost always enclosed by a wall, in the front generally a low one topped with decorative ironwork. Paths go straight to the front door and are usually of tiles, often patterned. As the front door is usually either to the extreme left or right there is a tiny border along the dividing wall on the one side. The actual garden area is invariably rectangular and overlooked by the main window of the drawing room, the contents of which would have been heavily concealed by lace curtains.

Those curtains reinforce the fact that front gardens were primarily for those who walk along the pavement. Putting to one side all the snobbery and one-upmanship that these horticultural showcases embodied, there is a wonderfully positive side to the concept; the house is set off by the garden and each garden is a contribution to the quality of life of the neighbourhood. The belief was held that each family should contribute to the overall delight of the urban environment. Sadly it is a legacy greatly under-appreciated today when many such front gardens, once the hard-won pride of their modest owners, the Pooters of the era, are abandoned, cemented over or left desolate and untended. A terrace of Victorian houses at the height of summer with their neatly ordered gardens ablaze with bloom must have lifted the spirits.

In re-creating such a garden I have adapted designs from Loudon's *The Gardener's Magazine* for 1835. The constant components of all front gardens throughout this period were grass, gravel, beds of geometric shape and the use of vertical focal points such as an ornament, or an exotic tree, a standard rose or evergreens.

The illustration (*right*) is an essay in ovals with a plant container (**1**) such as a tazza or an urn as a focal point. Originals in cast-iron, terracotta or other ceramic are still available but expensive. Fortunately, good reproductions are now being produced. It is filled with white pelargoniums.

The centre bed (**2**), which is a raised mound, has an edging of scallop shells (**3**). It could be bordered, as are the two long beds, with blue

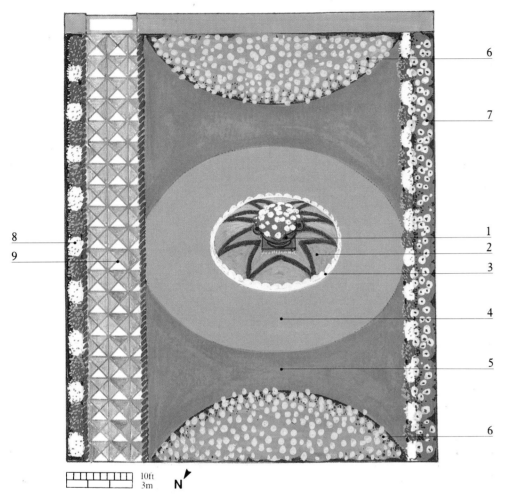

10ft
3m
N

lobelia and white alyssum. Within, it is carpet-bedded in a very simple way with two varieties of sempervivum. The bronzy-red star is delineated by the 'Commander Hay' variety, while the ground is filled with the ordinary common green type. Care must be taken to remove any attempts to flower. The more adventurous can experiment with other forms of dwarf or compact succulents, such as echeverias and sedum. The central oval bed is surrounded by an area of gravel (**4**) and lawn (**5**). The two semi-oval beds (**6**) are filled with the period classic, yellow calceolarias. The narrow border (**7**) which runs along one side of the garden is planted with another Victorian favourite, hollyhocks. White and yellow would be best, if you can find them. They will, of course, need staking. An even narrower border

(**8**) allows for another planting of lobelia and alyssum beside the tile path (**9**) that runs to the front door. The floral interest which is clearly lacking for the rest of the year might be made up if you extend the flowering season by planting the central bed with winter-flowering pansies and block plantings of tulips elsewhere.

VICTORIAN BEDDING SCHEMES

Victorian front gardens until the last couple of decades depended on bedding out. Although attacked by William Robinson (1838–1935) as early as the 1850s and later by Gertrude Jekyll, the bedding fashion continued into this century side by side with the new herbaceous borders. For a tiny front garden the bedding out principle in fact works wonderfully well. That format came in three variations. One was plain

bedding, literally the block planting of hardy, or half hardy annuals, and sometimes even perennials (pot grown and then planted out) into a single bed. Another was ribbon bedding, in which plants were arranged in stripes of colour, either in straight or wavy lines or in simple repeating patterns against a ground colour plant. The third was carpet-bedding, invented in 1868, which made use of foliage plants only, suppressing flowers, the plants literally being closely planted to form patterns akin to those on a Victorian carpet. As mosaiculture, it became very popular on the Continent.

The geometrically cut beds were often edged with silver plants such as *Antennaria dioica*, or with scarlet, yellow, blue or white flowers. The classic combination of white alyssum and blue lobelia emerged in the 1850s and continues to be popular to this day.

For a time, between about 1860 and 1880, it became fashionable to make use of the newly introduced sub-tropical plants such as canna hybrids, daturas, caladiums, bananas and, above all, hybrids, of *Begonia rex*. In these schemes, the tender plants used were valued for the colour and shape of their foliage and any flowers were removed during the season.

The interesting point about bedding schemes is that they can be varied from year to year in terms of plants and in those of colour and pattern. Those who would wish to pursue this subject in greater detail should consult the gardening books and magazines of the period which are full of schemes, often of daunting complexity.

Many varieties of plants used by the Victorians have been lost, or are now difficult to obtain. Some of their introductions have not stood the test of time, either because of the cost of the labour in raising the plants, or because they proved extremely invasive (for example *Cerastium tomentosum*, which was originally used to make a silver edging for beds). The main bedding plants still easily available for reasonably authentic period planting are: *Amaranthus caudatus* (love-lies-bleeding), *Antirrhinum majus* (common snapdragon), alyssum, calceolarias, clarkia, coreopsis, dahlias, *Dianthus chinensis* (Indian pink), eschscholzia, hyacinths, zonal pelargoniums, petunias, salvias, lobelia (both the low-growing blue-flowered varieties, as well as the tall scarlet lobelias), tulips, verbenas, polyanthus, pansies and violas.

The two most commonly used carpet-bedding plants in the nineteenth century were alternanthera and iresine, but more easily available alternatives would be echeverias, sedums and sempervivums.

EDWARDIAN
ROSE GARDEN

EDWARDIAN ROSE GARDEN

The rose garden in England is essentially a Regency creation. Although roses have been part of the garden repertory since classical antiquity, the development of a separate enclosure for the display of roses only begins to occur widely in the early nineteenth century, when the concept of a formal rose garden was first established. It had its roots, however, in the previous century in the style known as the gardenesque, which kept alive the tradition of the flower garden in spite of the dominance of the landscape style.

In the early eighteenth century only about fifty varieties of rose were known. They were planted in front of the shrubbery or as a separate rosarium at some distance from the house. These enclosures were formal in design, often focusing on the forerunner of our modern rockery, a piece of 'rockwork' on which dwarf and pendant types were grown, while the other roses were planted in groups to enable comparisons to be made, or grown as standards. Rose mania set in by 1800 because of the dramatic rise in the number of varieties, and Humphry Repton's revival of the formal garden in proximity to the house.

The enthusiasm for roses was encouraged by the introduction in the late eighteenth and early nineteenth centuries of repeat-flowering roses from China. Crosses between these and existing European varieties produced the Bourbons, the Portland roses and the Hybrid Perpetuals. By 1830 one London nursery could list no less than 1500 sorts of rose.

This proliferation coincided with Repton's interest in both the flower garden and in formality. It was Repton who began to create separate gardens for different types of plant and was the first garden designer to write about what we now call 'rooms'. One of his most famous series of such 'apartments' was at Ashridge in Hertfordshire, where, in 1815, he created no less than fifteen different types of garden. These included a rosary, the design for which he published in his *Fragments* (1816). The garden is circular, with a fountain at the centre and rose beds radiating out from it like flower petals; the whole is enclosed by a low trellis fence from which rose arches spring upwards.

The interest in rose gardens was also stimulated by the famous one planted in France for the Empress Josephine at Malmaison, near Haute-de-Seine, from 1798 onwards. Each bed contained a different variety of rose and visitors were led through the garden by a series of paths so that they could contemplate the beds in succession. Rambling roses figured prominently for the first time, deployed up pillars, arches and pergolas. In spite of the Napoleonic

wars this had enormous influence on the evolution and proliferation of rose gardens in England.

These early secluded rose gardens were filled with the old varieties recorded in the famous series of plates by Pierre-Joseph Redouté (1759 – 1841) who in his *Les roses* depicted those at Malmaison. Their colours were delicate and muted: pale pinks and whites, plum purples and velvety crimsons joined, by the middle of the century, by soft yellows. By the middle of the century these colours went out of fashion as Victorian taste entered its brilliant-bedding-plant phase. As a result the rose garden was pushed to a position away from the house and it was not until the close of the century, when the brilliant orange and scarlet varieties were introduced, that it was allowed to return to its former prominent position.

Gertrude Jekyll continued to advocate the rose garden as a separate entity, to be sited at some distance from the house, reiterating that in spite of the multiplication of repeat-flowering varieties, 'a rose garden can never be called gorgeous . . . the gorgeousness of brilliant bloom, fitfully arranged, is for other plants and other portions of the garden.' Miss Jekyll was the first exponent of a new attitude to roses. She approached them not as particular specimens to be collected but as components of beautiful garden pictures. To accord with this pictorialism, she recommended that roses should always be planted against a dark background to enhance their delicate colours, and that the plants should be cultivated for their luxuriance and beauty, not just for their size of bloom. She brought back into use the old roses — the Albas, the Damasks, the Centifolias and the Gallicas — and she also cultivated species roses. Her designs embraced the whole repertory of pergolas, arbours, pillars, arches, swags and garlands and she went on to recommend that any rigid formality should be broken by encouraging species roses and ramblers to scramble over fences, walls, trees and balustrading. It should not be forgotten that she welcomed many of the strong flame colours, the vivid oranges and scarlets, which have reached such a strength today that we have reacted against them.

The set of books which best captures the ethos of these gardens in their sunset glory — *Gardens Old and New* (1909), with photographs by Charles Latham — records the gardens of the great country houses with roses cascading in abundance over arches and pergolas or erupting in profusion from geometric beds. No one could have foreseen that these volumes would become memorials to a garden style which to all intents and purposes died in 1914.

THE EVOCATION
This garden is Jekyllesque in inspiration combining several elements from one of her most famous creations – the garden at Hestercombe in Somerset. It was the first time in her alliance with the architect Sir Edwin Lutyens that full scope was given to their collective imaginations. Hestercombe is a house set on a hillside with broad sweeping views out over Taunton Deane to the Blackdown Hills beyond. The design of 1906 centred on a large sunken parterre surrounded by raised walks and terraces with pergolas. It was not a rose garden, although roses figure among the plants that cover the pergolas. Away from the sunken parterre and in proximity to a fine orangery by Lutyens, Miss Jekyll designed what was called a Dutch garden of silver and grey foliage plants which spill out over a formal arrangement of beds inset into roughly cut local stone. These are the inspiration for the three circular enclosures (**1**) in the spandrels in my own design, which bring together a favourite Jekyll combination — still hugely popular today — of silver-grey plants with roses. The garden at Hestercombe has been under restoration by Somerset Council since 1973 and is the most complete available example of her art at its best.

The garden here is a quarter of a circle. It has a curved retaining wall (**2**) some 3 feet (1 metre) in height giving on to fields and country beyond. On the east and north sides, in true Jekyllesque vein, the garden is bounded by a yew hedge (**3**) interspersed with piers (**4**) at intervals and with an entrance (**5**) on the eastern side. It is perfectly possible to extend the design to a square by simply adding a fourth circular silver-grey enclosure into the missing spandrel.

In the centre of the garden there is an urn (**6**) or other garden ornament surrounded by a bed of catmint (**7**) whose soft billowing grey foliage and lavender flowers would soften the focal point and flop over the low containing hedge of clipped santolina (**8**). A lawn (**9**) stretches out to a circular pergola (**10**) of inexpensive larch poles, which straddles a path (**11**) edged on both sides with *Stachys lanata*. The pergola needs to be 7 or 8 feet (2 metres) in height to give clearance to walk beneath it and the larch poles must be robust and long enough to permit the omission of the supporting poles at junctions to the entrances and exits. All the roses in the garden are within a colour range of pink, white, buff or striped in those colours. Other colour themes are, of course, perfectly possible. The three circular spandrels are in brick and stone or crazy paving, as indeed is the pergola path. Their centre beds (**12**) contain low-growing silver-grey foliage plants which will not impede

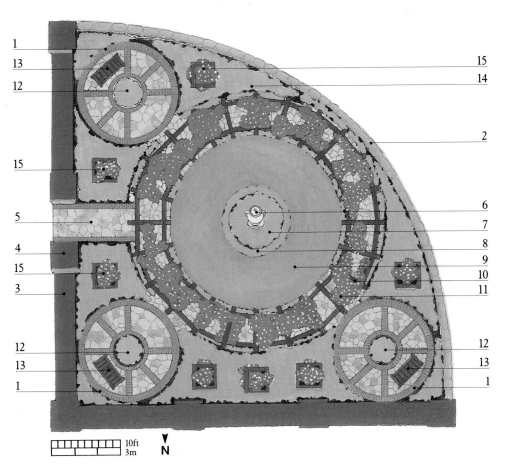

the view, plants such as lavender, ballota and artemisia; seats (**13**) are placed in the corners to enjoy the vistas. The remaining beds (**14**) have roses growing on larch-pole supports (**15**) and the beds are filled with larger, bolder silver-grey plants such as senecio or phlomis, which will give foliage interest all through the year.

EDWARDIAN ROSES

The National Trust in England has in its care most of the existing original and re-created Victorian and Edwardian rose gardens. Penelope Hobhouse in *A Book of Gardening* (1986) gives an excellent account of these gardens, their plans and planting, with a valuable discussion on the substitution of modern varieties of rose (which are more disease-resistant and flower for a far longer period) for the old ones but which still look correct for period.

Your ability to re-create accurately a pre-1914 rose garden will depend on access to a supplier which carries such stock. Of the roses Miss Jekyll used most, the following should still be available: for ramblers, 'The Garland' (1835), 'Mme Plantier' (1835) and 'Aimee Vibert' (1928) and, for the rose beds, 'Blanc Double de Coubert' (1892) and 'Mme Abel Chateney' (1895). Other favourites were: 'Mme Caroline Testout' (1890), 'Marie van Houtte' (1871), 'Lady Hillingdon' (1910), 'Hugh Dickson' (1905) and 'Frau Karl Druschki' (1901).

A good nursery specializing in old roses will carry several hundred varieties, and half the joy of planning a period rose garden is selecting the right combination of plants for shape, colour, scent and flowering season. The literature on old roses is vast but Graham Stuart Thomas's *The Old Shrub Roses* is a wonderful introduction to the subject by their greatest advocate. With our scheme of pink, buff and white I can give no more than a listing of some of the roses which I would choose:

For the pergola

'Félicité et Perpétue' (Rambler) (1827): large clusters of rather small creamy-white blooms; almost evergreen; mid-summer.

'Lady Waterlow' (Climbing Hybrid Tea) (1903): semi-double, soft-pink to salmon with deeper edges; robust climber.

'Mme Alfred Carrière' (Noisettiana) (Climbing) (1879): pinky-white to white clusters of double globular flowers: vigorous; good on a north wall.

'Mme Caroline Testout' (Climbing Hybrid Tea) (1870): vigorous climber of stain-pink with a deeper centre; huge strongly scented blooms.

'Mrs Herbert Stevens' (Climbing Hybrid Tea) (1910): white; fragrant; vigorous.

'Sanders White' (Rambler) (1912): rosette flowers of pure white in cascading clusters; bright green foliage.

'Tea Rambler' (Climber) (1904): clusters of salmon-pink, small, double flowers; fragrant; vigorous.

'The Garland' (Hybrid Musk) (1835): vigorous, spreading climber flowering early to mid-summer; masses of small semi-double, creamy-white almost daisy-like flowers tinged with pink; very fragrant.

'Gerbe Rose' (Climber) (1904): vigorous, large double flowers which open flat and soft pink; slight scent.

'May Queen' (Rambler) (1898): semi-double flowers of lilac-pink.

'Paul's Lemon Pillar' (Climbing Hybrid Tea) (1915): huge blooms of off-white suffused with lemon; scented; vigorous.

'Souvenir de la Malmaison' (Bourbon Climbing) (1893): lovely blush-white with face shaded in pink; scented; hates wet weather.

For the beds with larch supports

'Blanc Double de Coubert' (Rugosa) (1892): beautiful pure white, papery blooms; hips in the autumn.

'Alba Maxima' (Alba) (16th century): creamy-white with pink tints at the centre.

'Boule de Neige' (Bourbon) (1867): glossy foliage; full flowers of creamy-white; hips.

'Chapeau de Napoléon' (Centifolia: crested moss) (1826): rich pink.

'Zéphirine' Drouhin (Bourbon) (1868): semi-double, cerise-pink blooms.

'Louise Odier' (Bourbon) (1851): camellia-like, bright rose-pink flowers; vigorous.

'Great Maiden's Blush' (Alba) (earlier than the 15th century): blue-grey leaves; double, blush-pink flowers; strong scent.

'Mme Hardy' (Damascena) (1832): double, almost pure white flowers each with a green eye.

THE
REPERTORY
OF FORMALITY

L et us now turn to consider the various options open to those who wish to create a formal garden today. Bearing in mind the realities of the modern world, I am assuming: that the available space will be small — rarely more than a third of an acre (1500 square metres) and often much less; that financial resources will be limited, or have to be staggered over a number of years; and that, for the most part, the owner is his own gardener. These are the premises which have governed the compilation of this section as well as the designs which follow it in the next.

The repertory includes both a list of elements which it is possible to include in laying out a garden or part of a garden in the formal manner, and an examination of the options for their use. For each, I have outlined its place within the formal tradition and, at the same time, tried to give an indication of the labour and financial implications that might be involved — both necessary considerations when selecting ingredients for a garden. Topiary, for instance, is a surprisingly inexpensive and low-maintenance garden art, thanks to modern machinery, though it requires a large input of patience; flower gardens, on the other hand, although delightful and quick to mature, can be costly and labour-intensive.

The aim of the repertory is also to illustrate some remarkably successful contemporary examples of formality, each offering an idea or statement on a particular topic. Some of the illustrations give views of complete gardens which could easily be adapted to other sites. The simplicity and freshness of the little Dutch water garden (page 69) is an instance, so, too, is the tiny rose garden (page 83) whose arches and simple paving pattern provide the ideal framework for billowing clouds of pink and white blossom. And who of those wanting a vegetable garden would not be tempted to emulate the Swiss potager (page 96) with its picket fence and enchanting geometric beds of produce and flowers? Other views focus on delightful details such as the lozenges of box (page 93) containing culinary herbs which could be adapted for a plot outside almost any kitchen door, provided it faced south. Anyone with a garden seat will find it hard to resist topiary sentinels (page 66), and you can find a wealth of planting ideas, such as the unexpected marriage of pink roses and *Sedum spectabile* (page 77), or hostas dappling and defining a shady avenue with rare taste (page 81).

Here, in short, are some of the best formal gardens of today, living testaments to the year-round pleasures of formality seen not only in spring and summer but in autumn and winter too. They demonstrate the vitality of the tradition and its ability — not always recognized — to be adapted to contemporary living. All the gardens here were made during this century, many during the last fifteen years. Virtually any of them is attainable within such a timespan from its first planting. That should be inspiration indeed.

◀ A stately vista along a path, through a gazebo and hedging, across a shimmering pond to a bust on a plinth.
▲ A sculptural focal point, low hedges defining the spaces, and an interesting use of espaliered fruit trees as a screen.

PARTERRES AND KNOTS

◀ This knot, an incident in a larger garden, based on one in *L'Agriculture et la Maison Rustique* (1583), is 12 feet (4 metre) square and made up of green and golden dwarf box intertwining a lozenge of germander, with a large ball of *Phillyrea angustifolia* at the centre. At the points where the hedges interlace, they are carefully clipped so that they seem to go over and under one another.

▶ The problems of a long narrow town garden are solved completely by a parterre whose curving baroque patterns can be appreciated from the main reception rooms on the first floor. Colour is added by infilling the compartments with flowers in season. The austere formality of the garden as a whole is broken by the cascade of foliage from the trees and shrubs on either side.

The parterre — a decorative garden laid out in a symmetrical geometric pattern on one level — has been part of the design repertory of the garden for five hundred years, and it is as effective today as when it was first invented. In the seventeenth century it evolved into distinct forms: the *parterre de broderie*, or embroidered parterre, which was a pattern usually made of box filled in with turf and coloured earths (see pages 38–9), while the English form, the *parterre à l'anglaise*, consisted of simple geometrically shaped areas of turf with a statue in the middle of the composition. If the turf was cut into an elaborate pattern it was known as *gazon coupé*. Parterres were ousted from favour by the landscape movement in the eighteenth-century style but were revived again in the last century.

Knots, which historically preceded parterres, are patterns made by continuous bands of plants interwoven with each other. The plants used included thyme, rosemary, box and germander, but the pattern of a sixteenth-century knot could as easily have been formed from old bones, tiles and pebbles. By the beginning of the seventeenth century the term had lost its original meaning and a knot became simply a description of one quarter of a rectilinear garden laid out in four quarters dissected by straight paths. Today the word is used to mean any kind of formal arrangement in dwarf box or planting that is based, however loosely, on one of the early seventeenth-century knot designs.

As garden forms, knots and parterres still have a validity today, although both usually depend on historical designs. I have never seen a contemporary knot but it would be perfectly possible to invent one. Parterres need not be made only in the flowing baroque idiom and I have deliberately included designs based on Art Deco

sources as well as on Op Art and abstract paintings (pages 128–31). There are great possibilities in reviving the *parterre à l'anglaise*, especially as the maintenance would be easy. An Art Nouveau or Op Art *parterre à l'anglaise* would be quite a startling innovation, and I can think of few better settings for a piece of contemporary sculpture.

It is not always possible to look down on parterres and knots but it is traditional to do so, and encourages appreciation of the symmetry of the pattern — especially when the formality is reinforced by a spring and summer planting in blocks of colour. If you prefer, you can decide not to plant at all and fill the shapes made between the hedging with coloured gravels or sand instead. Or you could temper the severity of the pattern with an informal planting of, for instance, fairly tall roses that will arch over the hedges softening their rigid lines.

The effects of light on the walls and surfaces of a parterre are essential to its success. Watch the movement of the sun when planning one, and consider its effect on your scheme. Light will animate and define a parterre's walls, enclosures and patterns in a startling and dramatic way. Light, too, will highlight the textural quality of the hedging plants, the furry softness of santolina or the tiny shiny leaves of box.

These various alternatives call for different amounts of garden work through the year, from a simple knot which only needs a minimal annual feeding and clipping, to a parterre overflowing with seasonal flowers which is a highly labour-intensive commitment. The exhilarating feature of both is that its pattern is there to enjoy from the moment it is planted. Within about five to eight years it will have matured into a work of art.

▶ The design for this unusual informal hexagonal open knot is taken from William Lawson's *The New Orchard and Garden* (1618). The pattern is a six-pointed star of Jerusalem, composed of two interlinking triangles, one of green dwarf box and the other of silvery-grey santolina. A bushy hedge of dwarf lavender links the points of the star. Within this configuration there is a soft mixed low planting in pink, pale yellow and white. The tiny statue of a putto in the centre might be set off to better advantage if it were placed on a pedestal.

◀ A sunburst of box-edged beds encircles a sundial as a focal point. The hedging gives firm structure to a mixed herbaceous planting in pink, blue and white. This pattern of beds would also lend itself well to block planting in the spring with tulips, followed by bedding plants during the summer months. It would also make an excellent herb garden.

▶ In a recently planted 30-foot (9-metre) square knot the geometry is of the simplest: an inner and outer square of box, intersected by a circle and four semi-circles. It provides a strong framework in which to display a collection of plants, many of which came from America and were known to the two John Tradescants, father and son, gardeners to Charles I and his queen, Henrietta Maria.

▲ Quite substantial existing trees can be incorporated into a rigidly formal enclosure without impairing the overall scheme. The old tree here in no way disturbs the classic symmetry of this parterre, whose maintenance would be minimal. Four box-edged beds surround a tiny fountain and four massive yew cones give monumental balance, shape and height; they also provide a dramatic contrast to the woodland backcloth beyond the enclosure. Each quarter is carpeted with an evergreen groundcover which bulbs can happily penetrate in spring.

▲ ▲ Beautiful bold Baroque scrollwork shows the dramatic effects which can be obtained with box hedging of varying widths. Careful thought must always be given to the mowing implications of such a scheme. These problems could be avoided by using coloured gravels instead of grass. This would be historically correct and would then need only extremely careful application of weed killer from time to time.

▲ An attempt to reconstruct a late seventeenth-century *parterre à l'anglaise* seen here shortly after planting. Two lines of box hedging delineate the compartments which are filled with grass. There are no vertical accents or flowers in this garden which relies entirely on flat pattern to achieve its effect.

▲ ▲ A most unusual box parterre on a huge scale frames a lawn with bold lozenge-shaped compartments inset with yew domes and standards of *Prunus lusitanica*. Essentially it replaces the space more usually occupied by a shrubbery or herbaceous border, both of which are often labour-intensive, with an easily maintained frame of architectural greenery. The effect could be easily copied on a smaller scale.

▲ This knot was designed in 1980. It is made of box and germander with a containing hedge of santolina. The areas inside the hedges are only partly gravelled, to allow for the planting of such enchanting details as the bouquet of sops-in-wine or dianthus. It is interesting to compare this knot with the one pictured on page 54, which used the same source, and note the differences in scale and training.

▲ ▲ For a very simple box parterre beneath an old apple tree, four quarters are divided by a brick path with a large flower pot at the centre. The random planting acts as a foil to the formal framework.

This pattern could be adapted to a smaller site, where it would make a complete garden design in itself; but you would need to add height to the centrepiece to compensate for the loss of the larger setting and old fruit trees.

▲ American formality often seems to have an attractive informality about it. Here the familiar dwarf box is used but it is loosely trimmed to give a rounded profile that is quite distinct from the dense and sharp angularity of its European counterpart.

▲ ▲ Gravel within a parterre can provide a stronger contrast than grass to its surrounding dwarf box hedging; this is seen to be true when this parterre is compared with the ones shown opposite on the far left. The pattern with vertical accents in ordinary box is repeated on either side of the central path.

▲ A small box parterre focuses on a stone urn with the Baroque scroll pattern repeated in each of the four corners. The urn would look better if it was set off by more handsome and luxuriant planting at the base of the plinth. In the box parterre itself a few standard roses, or rose obelisks, symmetrically placed would add attractive height.

◀ In summer the light is warm and strong on a parterre, the greens fresh and luscious. Flowers extend the palette range, which can be changed year by year if bedding plants are used. Here a parterre of grass-filled curves gains summer contrast from a central bed of begonias. The composition preserves the exalted status of good cut grass as it was in the seventeenth century, when close-cut turf was not to be trodden on but appreciated aesthetically as much as the flowers.

▲ No season brings out the virtues of a parterre better than winter when the structural geometry will give pleasure even on the dullest day and, on the brightest, will positively sparkle. Winter reveals the importance of sculptural features to draw the eye in the absence of flowers, it also brings out the contrast of the solid hedging elements against the spidery pattern of shrub and tree branches; and it invites a mature appreciation of a more subtle colour palette. Seen under snow, a parterre can be a dazzling sight, looking as though it were made of icing sugar. Fortunately box is robust enough to withstand substantial falls of snow.

TOPIARY

▲ Traditional specimen topiary, of a kind produced and admired by the Arts and Crafts Movement, symmetrically flanks the entrance path to a thatched cottage. It would take at least fifteen years to bring such pieces to their full outline, but the result would be unique and could only improve year by year as the foliage increases in density.

▶ Simple, perfectly geometrical topiary shapes give vertical emphasis to a box parterre in the swirling French Baroque style. At either end of the design box cones arise from compartments, and at the centre there is a box ball. Even devoid of its summer planting the overall effect remains deeply satisfying in terms of pattern and light and shade.

Topiary is the art of pruning and cutting plants to shape. Its variety, both of shapes attainable and of suitable plants, is potentially enormous. You can use trees and shrubs such as arbor-vitae (*Thuja*), juniper (*Juniperus*), yew (*Taxus baccata*), *Phillyrea*, holly (*Ilex*), firethorn (*Pyracantha*), privet (*Ligustrum*), and box (*Buxus sempervirens*), as well as garden plants that respond to the shears and secateurs, such as lavender (*Lavendula*), rosemary (*Rosmarinus*), lavender cotton (*Santolina*), germander (*Teucrium*), and even ivy (*Hedera*) which can be trained to clothe pre-formed wire frames. It is wrong to associate topiary, as is commonly done, only with its most complex expression, the training of specimen pieces such as a chess set in yew. Any clipping to attain a particular shape comes within the definition of topiary. It is easy to forget that all ornamental hedging is fundamentally topiary too.

Topiary has been part of the garden repertory since at least Roman times. In the first century AD Pliny the Younger described whole scenes sculpted from cypress, and the use of box to form the name of the owner of the villa. Although the art existed in the Middle Ages, usually practised on single specimens in pots, its real revival took place in fifteenth-century Italy. The *Hypnerotamachia Polyphili* (1499) contains the first printed designs for topiary, and was to have considerable influence on garden design throughout the century. From Italy the popularity of topiary in one form or another spread across Europe.

Topiary training as the essence of formal garden architecture, however, belongs especially to France in the seventeenth century; there, entire gardens were composed from hedges of varying heights combined with single geometric shapes cut from evergreens such as yew, holly, box, laurel, bay and phillyrea.

During the next century, with the landscape style holding predominance over garden design, topiary came to represent all that was out of fashion. Much of it was swept away, especially in Britain but even in Europe, despite the continuing vitality of the formal tradition there — particularly in Italy, France and Holland. In Britain an interest in topiary was revived in the nineteenth century, and, as a result, our idea of topiary in England today is based, mistakenly, on groups of exotic shapes found in Victorian cottage gardens. Because of the dislocation of two world wars, the lack of labour and changes in gardening fashion, topiary virtually passed into oblivion for more than half a century. Only in recent years have there been serious stirrings to revive this almost defunct garden art in its more elaborate forms. Fortunately, the vicissitudes of the status of topiary in Britain were not so strongly felt in America, where it developed its own idioms and momentum in response to local climate. Gardens that made extensive use of topiary continued to be made or re-created from the beginning of the century, from the Villa Vizcaya in Miami and the gardens of Thomas Brayton in Rhode Island to Filoli in California.

Topiary can figure in the formal garden today in many forms, from a single specimen to an entire design governed by arrangements of clipped hedges. Modern mechanical clippers have revived the option of creating really ambitious hedges. Single specimens will inevitably be more demanding at the training stage but the result will be well worth the investment.

▶ Simple box cones and low-growing standards provide vertical punctuation marks within a parterre. The self-seeded foxgloves do not upset the architecture of the design which is a mirror image pattern flanking a central path from the house.

▼ The American contribution to the topiary tradition is seen here in a re-created garden of the eighteenth century at Williamsburg in Virginia. These unsophisticated small town gardens have a wonderful freshness and domesticity about them, expressed in details such as this hen sitting on her eggs in the midst of one of the beds.

▶ Box cones and standards feature in a re-creation of a parterre originally laid out in 1701 and which has now been re-planted. Its original appearance is recorded in a view of about 1707. Each section of the parterre is 48 feet (14.6 metres) square and the box-edged beds are filled with variegated and purple sage, *Festuca ovina* var. *Glauca*, *Echium creticum*, *Calendula officinalis*, *Lilium pyrenaicum*, and *Iberis sempervirens*. The symmetry of the garden is continued beyond the parterre with the four Portugal laurel (*Prunus lusitanica*) pruned into umbrella-shaped trees.

Reduced in scale this would make a pretty small garden: you could replace the labour-intensive turf with paving or gravel paths.

◀ A pair of box spirals—triumphs of the topiarist's art—add symmetry to a garden seat placed to perfection against a wall hung with clematis. Box spirals like these would be a long-term project but faster-growing yew cones, or two spirals of trained ivy would make a similar statement.

▼ A pair of Portugal laurel (*Prunus lusitanica*) trained as mopheads flank a garden seat, acting, at certain times of day, as elegant sunshades and bringing perfect balance to the tableau.

Trees trained as mopheads or umbrellas are an ideal means adding height and substance to a small garden without the problems, particularly of shade, of a full-size tree.

◀ A most ingenious garden arch has been created in a hedge of beech—a relatively fast-growing plant and more susceptible to training than is generally recognized.

◀ Yew will always remain the queen of hedging plants for the creation of evergreen architecture and the provision of an ideal foil for flowers. Such a majestic tableau as this might take fifteen years or more to come into its prime but the result justifies the waiting.

◀ A bird sculpted from *Lonicera nitida* in a pot proves the potential of portable topiary as a highlight or focal point. Dutch and Belgian nurseries grow and export whimsical topiary of this kind, the taste of which can be variable.

WATER

◀ The use of water as a *miroir d'eau*, reflecting the clouds and sky and two stone baskets of fruit, holds this small garden together in tranquility. The balanced planting on either side contributes to a scene of total harmony.

▶ A modern version of the classic *parterre d'eau* lays out rectangles of water in a formal arrangement, clipped box, brick and stone reminiscent of a painting by Mondrian. The deployment of water like a miniature canal emphasizes the lines of perspective.

Water has figured in garden designs since antiquity, but it was only in the Renaissance that a distinctive repertory for the formal garden emerged, when advances in hydraulic engineering made it possible to convey water huge distances and maintain a pressure strong enough for the most ambitious 'water tricks' or *guochi d' acqua*, as they were called. When the new skill in controlling water was harnessed to the new advances in architecture and sculpture, the combination resulted in the rapid development of every form of fountain, cascade, grotto and canal. Throughout the Renaissance and Baroque periods the manipulation of water on a grand scale was to be fundamental to all garden design.

In the formal garden tradition water was deployed in one of two ways. The first and more subtle use was as a static feature; divided into unruffled surfaces that reflected buildings or the sky, it was known as a *miroir d'eau* or *parterre d'eau*. The famous water parterre of the mid-sixteenth century at the Villa Lante at Bagnaia, Italy, was one of the prototypes, as was the Grand Canal at Versailles, France, made in the middle of the following century. Infinitely more showy was the other way of using water: as continuous movement, spurting upwards or cascading downwards, catching the light. It was often designed to flow in set sculptural tableaux; with river gods and goddesses as its source, it went on to embrace the entire garden as it cascaded downwards in a heavy torrent or in the thinnest of veils, or was thrown upwards again by a figure such as Neptune.

Such grandiose traditions obviously cannot be emulated in the small gardens of today, but water can be used enormously successfully even in the most modest formal schemes. Perhaps the most effective deployment of water is to create a *miroir d'eau* whose prime function is to reflect the sky, and the house or a garden building. This treatment has a classic purity in the grand tradition, in which geometric areas of water were appreciated solely for their refractive quality. It is typified by the seventeenth-century Dutch canal garden, where a gazebo placed at one end would be reflected in its entirety in the water, to the onlooker's lasting pleasure.

Such elegance is sadly lacking today, when ponds are usually planted with water lilies and other aquatic plants. The passion for turning water into liquid flowerbeds is a recent innovation. In the examples illustrated on the following pages, in most of which there is some planting, it would be interesting to consider the effect of leaving the surface of the water entirely uncluttered. That treatment might better serve the prime objective of sheets of water in formal garden design — to act as shimmering mirrors of light, and as reflectors of a garden's most beautiful structures. If your desire is to grow a bed of aquatic plants, treat it as you would any other flowerbed; but it has no real place in the formal tradition of water in garden design.

A design involving moving water can never be more than modest in scale in a small garden: a trickle of water from a mask head set into a wall, for instance, or a jet animating the surface of a pond; and even with all today's gadgetry, water involves a heavy capital outlay and constant maintenance. But as a focal point, there is little more appealing than the sight and sound of moving water. The advantage of the formal treatment of water is that it never pretends to be anything other than total artifice.

▼ A beautifully proportioned small pond is marred by a clutter of plants which obviate its reflective qualities and upset its symmetry. The removal of the statue of Venus de Medici would clarify the vista beyond.

◀ An obelisk wall fountain embowered in variegated ivy makes a perfect termination to a garden vista.

Wall fountains can be the ideal way of bringing water into a small garden because, unlike the fountain forms, they are by nature small in scale.

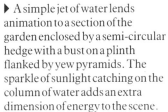
▶ A simple jet of water lends animation to a section of the garden enclosed by a semi-circular hedge with a bust on a plinth flanked by yew pyramids. The sparkle of sunlight catching on the column of water adds an extra dimension of energy to the scene.

▼ Water used as a mirror for light is aligned to a window of the house. Seen from that window, the formal nature of the design would be even clearer, thanks to the symmetrical placing of the terracotta pots, the flanking balls of box and the low soft planting in grey-greens. There is also a pretty vista to a garden seat.

▶ In a garden of bold simplicity, strong axes are created by a pleached lime avenue stretching into the distance with a counter axis in the form of an oblong canal placed so that it mirrors the avenue. The contrast between the shimmering water and the verdant green of the grass adds to the success of the scheme.

▼ A highly successful formal treatment of what might be described as a water flowerbed is completed with box hedging. This is a perfectly legitimate garden feature but makes little if any use of the water's prime quality of reflection.

▶ A vista leads the eye through a window and across stepping stones in a small canal which runs along one side of the house. The view is enhanced by symmetrical planting.

▼ A rectangular raised pond conceived from the outset as a bed for aquatic plants is placed to complement the beds of other flowers in proximity to it.

FLOWER GARDENS

▲ In a formal flower garden the beds are planted deliberately to reinforce the basic geometry with pattern, using only deep purple–blue and white flowers. The effect would be dull if the planting were only of one colour. The addition of the white flowers, especially as they pick up the pale colour in the blue ones, brings the scheme to life. The sense of controlled pattern would be lost if there were dramatic changes in height between the plants.

▶ The informal mixed planting in the Jekyllesque border is given firm structure by the clipped conifers. They add formal accents which also emphasize the vista. If the green colonnade was removed, the border would lack contrast, and the sense of vista would be greatly diminished.

The flower garden has a history both as a formal and an informal entity. Its strictly formal history is inextricably linked with that of the parterre, since flowers were grown only in parterres or in the narrow beds that flanked them, in any formal garden scheme from the seventeenth century until geometric beds were revived in the Victorian period. The history of the informal flower garden began in the eighteenth century when the delights of flowers were rediscovered in reaction to the excesses of the landscape style which had swept flower gardens away and brought grass right up to the windows of the house.

The newfangled informal flower gardens also developed partly in response to the exaltation of the natural garden by the French philosopher Rousseau. The most famous example was at Nuneham Park in Oxfordshire, England (begun 1771), in which irregularly shaped beds, each crammed with blossom, were scattered across the grass beneath the trees. The passion for flowers was further fuelled in the next century both by the trophies of plant hunters who brought home thousands of new varieties from all over the world, and by Loudon's exhortation to revive formal gardens with their geometric bedding schemes. The new formality, in turn, was to be assailed by William Robinson (1838–1935) in his famous book *The English Flower Garden* (1883), in which he extolled the virtues of the informal garden planted with drifts of softly coloured perennials and with plants clambering up the walls. That book went into sixteen editions, the last appearing as late as 1956. His hugely pervasive influence was reinforced by his great disciple, Gertrude Jekyll, in the three hundred or so gardens she designed. Robinson and Jekyll remain the dominant forces in the approach to planting flower gardens even today.

It may be questionable to draw a distinction at all between parterres and flower gardens; yet it does seem useful to divide those formal gardens whose prime intention is to display the garden's architectural geometric structure from those whose aim is to provide a firm framework for a massive display of flowers within the Robinsonian–Jekyllesque tradition. It should be remembered that traditional herbaceous borders were treated as formal elements of the garden. They were generally placed either side of a path, itself forming a vista, and were backed by firm architectural walls or hedges which displayed the flowers to advantage. Within the borders sensitive massing of flowers could produce a finely balanced tonality. There are still lessons to be learnt from this when using flowers to make a formal garden. A path, for instance, makes a stronger statement of perspective if it is bordered on either side by an identical planting, say of catmint or lavender, backed by a haze of blue flowers — geums, violas, delphiniums, scabious and lupins. You can introduce formal accents even in the most informal herbaceous borders merely, for example, by siting clumps of one prominent perennial equidistant from another.

Flower gardens are for the really dedicated gardener. They are extremely hard — though rewarding — work, requiring constant attention to detail in order to maintain through the flowering months a succession of bloom which will compose into a balanced garden picture. As both Robinson and Jekyll knew, such a balance is more likely to be achieved within a formal outline.

◀ A rare instance of a formal garden composed almost entirely of herbaceous plants, with focal points created by more solid shrubby plants. In winter the formal structure will be less apparent. These flowers are planted to give the effect of a loose undulating hedge containing the areas of lawn in summer. Softness of colour is an essential ingredient of its success.

◀ A yew hedge frames a simple garden of beds edged with box, in which pink roses are most unusually combined with a border of *Sedum spectabile*. A great deal of the success of this little garden depends on the contrast its controlled formality makes to the splendour of the natural woodland beyond. Without such a dramatic backdrop the planting would need to be made far more interesting.

▲ A modest mixed planting of roses and herbaceous plants, such as foxgloves and lupins, acquires order and a sense of space from the containing hedge and gravel path. Distance is heightened by a balanced planting of pink flowers flanking a vista to soft blues and yellows. Notice the care which has been taken in graduating the height of the plants, both permanent and seasonal, to accentuate the sense of recession.

◀ This tiny formal flower garden has been successfully carried out with the most slender of means: pre-cast concrete slabs for the path, a modest terracotta pot to draw the eye and a wooden seat to close the vista. Lavender contains the flowerbeds, which are filled with a mixed planting of roses and assorted herbaceous plants.

▲ Another delightful tiny flower garden, also with a vista to a seat, is enclosed by a young green hedge that provides the ideal backcloth for beds symmetrically planted with multi-coloured spring flowers: crown imperials, tulips, narcissi and rhododendrons.

◀◀ This path is transformed into a spectacular and inviting vista through its identical symmetrical planting of red and white roses with a generous edging of lavender. It has made superb use of the two magnificent ancient yews which must precede the path by decades in date. Without the yews, the vista would call for a glorious gate or gate piers to draw the eye down the path.

◀ The interest of this very beautiful and unusual perspective is dramatically heightened by the ravishing flanking carpets of different varieties of hosta. Few shady walks could be done with better style and taste.

This is a single effect in a large garden. In a small one its interest could be extended in spring by snowdrops and hardy crocus and in autumn by drifts of cyclamen.

ROSE GARDENS

◀ A rose garden in the form of a box parterre filled with pale pink roses. Box topiary provides a symmetrical architectural framework and vertical accents, while a pergola gives added height and vista.

▶ A rose garden articulated by brick paths and cubes of box with clematis-covered cross-arches, and a robust pot as a focal point. The colour is confined to white and pink beautifully set off against the dark green hedge.

Rose gardens were an invention of the nineteenth century (see page 51). Like herb gardens, their impact is seasonal. If the roses are of the old-fashioned varieties, such as the albas and gallicas, the season will be confined to four to six weeks of splendour in mid-summer. Even if they are repeat-flowering types, such as the hybrid perpetuals and modern varieties, that period does not extend beyond autumn. Roses without leaves are unsightly plants (hence the traditional siting of a separate rose garden out of the main view of the house); it is therefore essential to place them within a scheme which will have independent value during the non-flowering months. A formal structure is the ideal solution, for decorative plant supports and evergreen architecture will give interest through all four seasons.

A dark green hedge, preferably of yew, is the perfect background to most colours, but especially to white, pink and pale yellow blooms. Box topiary and hedging likewise provide both a refreshing contrast and, at the same time, strong architectural form for the entire year. The same is true of handsome pergolas and rose supports in the form of arches, obelisks and garlands for climbers, ramblers and pillar roses. (Many of these architectural supports are now prefabricated and are available in a great variety of shape and size.) And further interest could be added by a judicious siting of urns, tubs or statuary to provide accent or to emphasize a vista.

Great care should be taken in the control of colour and its allocation within the beds in order to achieve a harmonious and balanced picture. The hot reds, yellows and oranges of some of the recently introduced varieties are unsettling, unless used in moderation and offset by an abundant massing of white and creamy blooms. If height is not added by other elements, include a symmetrical grouping of standards.

Other planting should set the roses off to advantage while they are in flower, besides being of intrinsic interest at other periods. The classic combination remains silver and grey foliage plants: lavender (*Lavandula*), lavender cotton (*Santolina chamaecyparissus*), catmint (*Nepeta*) or *Stachys lanata* 'Silver Queen' for edging or dividing the beds, with the helichrysums, artemisias and sages, especially *Salvia officinalis* 'Purpurascens', within. Other possibilities are the lime-green *Alchemilla mollis* with its dew-hugging leaves for goundcover and, if you have rose supports, clematis. To prolong flowering interest roses can be underplanted with a sprinkling of common snowdrops (*Galanthus nivalis*), hardy crocuses (*Crocus tommasinianus*) and water-lily tulips (*Tulipa kaufmanniana*), all of which are best left undisturbed to multiply for the spring. Lavender-coloured violas and blue myosotis can equally be used to advantage.

In an age of container-grown plants, you can be deceived into thinking that an instant rose garden is possible. A successful formal rose garden is a ten- to fifteen-year commitment, because the evergreen components of it are as vitally important as any of the roses. Few sights are more depressing than beds of rose bushes without any verdant architecture to help display them to their full glory. Yet few sights are more ravishing than a well-structured rose garden in full bloom; with perhaps a scented rose bower to sit in, and with roses of different heights and hues, shapes and scents to captivate the senses, even the few short weeks of resplendence will repay the work of pruning and tying, fertilizing and spraying.

◀ A splendid embowered eye-catcher on a scale bold enough to hold any formal rose garden together in terms of focal point and vista.

▼ A symmetrical arrangement of box-edged beds gives much-needed structure to contain and articulate a mixed bold planting with red roses at the front of the borders. The solitary standard rose is a weak element in the composition.

◀ A parterre rose garden designed by Sir Edwin Lutyens and originally planted by Gertrude Jekyll but now re-planted in blocks of colour. A garden of great style with a marvellous descent into it which enhances the strong use made of perspective leading the eye into the surrounding landscape. An urn acts as a focal point. The addition of a few standards in the spandrels would help to give some height to the overall composition.

▶ An informal rose vista in soft shades of pale pink and yellow leading to a pair of fastigiate Irish yews which make an entrance to a lawn beyond. Box hedging and topiary flank the path, and lead the eye onwards.

▼ A panoramic view of the same garden as that seen on page 83 reveals much more of its elegant overall design; the clever use of portable focal points beneath the clematis-clad arches, the deliberate placing of only white roses in the centre beds with pink assigned to the surrounding ones and the importance of an evergreen backdrop. All the axes in this essentially simple garden are interesting.

◀ A row of metal arches
supporting sprawling red roses
forms an inviting vista. The
formality is accentuated by a
symmetrical placing of two tall box
cones in tubs which act as sentinels
at the entrance; and the course of
the vista is followed through by
Versailles tubs containing
standard fuchsias arranged in
pairs.

PAVED GARDENS

▲ A paved passage is transformed into a little town garden with a vista of treillage enriched with climbers alternating with container-grown shrubs and topiary cut from a golden variety of *Cupressus*.

▶ A delightful paved back garden glimpsed through fronds of giant euphorbia symmetrically arranged around a focal point of a stone basket of fruit arising from a bed of *Lamium*. Low maintenance has been a premium in this garden's planning with a lavish use of perennials, many of them evergreen. Restricting the palette to green, but then using every shade from the lime of the *Alchemilla mollis* to the dense dark green ivy, contributes to the feeling of harmony and tranquillity.

Small gardens that are either entirely or almost entirely paved make up an indefinable yet nevertheless recognizable category of gardens. These vary from the tiny paved yards of terraced town houses in cooler countries, through a great many front gardens — which are often given over completely to paving, to some of the greatest masterpieces of garden art in this genre which belong to the Islamic tradition with its delicate use of rivulets, fountains and sheets of water. But the paved garden belongs most typically to those places where climate rules out grass and where the key objectives of protection from the sun and the provision of shade are best met by paved courtyards and cloisters.

There are both practical and aesthetic reasons for deciding to pave a major part of a small garden, particularly when heat and lack of water would mean huge difficulty in maintaining the quality of even a small area of turf. In any climate, paving has the advantage of requiring virtually no maintenance; and in small gardens which have to contend with the considerable wear and tear of frequent traffic, paving can provide an ideal solution.

Paving is just as valid a surface as grass. It, too, responds to the play of light and to the change in seasons, in a very different but no less exciting way. Well chosen materials and care taken in their arrangement can form the basis, with minimal planting, of a really distinguished garden. By their very nature, paved gardens have a tendency to be formal, and it is worth exploiting these formal qualities to make a balanced and harmonious composition.

There is a very wide choice of materials available; when you make your plans, try to include as much really good-quality material as you can afford. Your selection should be based not only on economic and practical considerations — such as resistance to frost-damage — but also on aesthetic ones. Look at the colours and textures of the materials of the architecture of your house and decide how you can best complement them — by a close match or a complete contrast. Natural and man-made materials can often be successfully combined, and can enhance one another, but take great care in your choice of the latter, as much that is currently on the market is in questionable taste.

In designing the paved garden, the proportion devoted to hard surface, as opposed to beds for flowers and other plants, can be varied according to your needs and the time available. Even within a small paved garden there is generally room for beds of shrubs, roses or other flowers, herbs and even vegetables and fruit. And an enormously attractive feature of any paved garden would be an appropriate use of water — a small pool or fountain.

In planning a paved formal garden you must carefully consider how much commitment you are ready to make. Be honest with yourself. If you are looking for minimal maintenance, concentrate your energies on making the paving as interesting as possible and reduce the horticultural input to groundcover plants and those which virtually look after themselves. Use the plants to focus attention on a really original paving pattern or a mosaic. If, on the other hand, you intend to devote a great deal of time to the garden, do the reverse: have simple paving to set off a varied and magnificent display of flowers and foliage. Both approaches have equal validity and can result in gardens of real distinction and style.

▶ A delicious tiny southern courtyard garden has a vista through white flowers along a beautiful tessellated path to a shady pavilion. A mirror has been positioned so that it both reflects light into the pavilion and optically increases the length of the vista.

◀ A paved terrace enclosed by a box hedge makes an alfresco dining room with an architectural treillage to enliven a dull wall. The box hedge defines the dining room's boundary and the cones its door.

▼ ◀ A courtyard garden of gravel walks and box-edged beds has a 'moat' to cross from the house.

▼ A raised pond with a comfortable ledge on which to sit is the central feature of this formal paved enclosure. The bold curve of the entrance arch echoes that of the pond, an essential design point.

HERB GARDENS

▲ This herb garden fills a large walled enclosure in the simplest way. The space is divided symmetrically into rectangles by gravel paths; a pergola at the crossing is decked with honeysuckle; and seats have been placed from where vistas can be enjoyed. Large beds edged with a substantial box hedge contain medicinal plants and traditional herbs as well as roses and flowers of a kind known when the original garden was created at the very end of the seventeenth century.

▶ This herb garden is one element in a far larger garden, but of a design that could be easily adapted. It is a long narrow strip 45 feet (14 metres) long, by 6 feet (1.8 metres) wide, flanking a pathway leading from the kitchen door. The herbs are contained within a simple repeating pattern of five castellated lozenges of dwarf box, with 2-foot- (60-centimetre) - high box cones at either end to provide vertical emphasis. Each bed has more than one variety of herb.

The herb garden goes back to classical antiquity and was one of the few forms of gardening to survive through the Dark Ages. Since herbs were grown essentially for their medicinal and culinary properties they found protection within the monastic cloister, along with a few plants, such as roses and honeysuckle, that were grown for perfume and decoration. The herbs cultivated were usually rosemary, marjoram, thyme, sage, parsley and mint. Larger collections might also include tarragon, fennel, dill, chervil, lovage, rue and lemon balm, besides many others. From the start, their arrangement tended to be formal, in geometric beds that were often edged with low hedging plants.

From the Renaissance onwards herbs became part of the physic garden and the potager — a tradition we can still see today in the great physic gardens across Europe, such as those established in the mid-sixteenth century at Padua and, at the end of that century, in Montpellier. It was not until this century that the fashion emerged of creating a separate ornamental herb garden. The real impetus for this came between the wars, from the writings of Eleanour Sinclair Rohde (1882–1950) on the medicinal nature of sixteenth-century gardens. She planted the first notably formal herb garden, a chequerboard, at Lullingstone Castle in Kent, England. Vita Sackville-West's herb garden at Sissinghurst, also in Kent, planted in 1947, was to have an even greater influence. The ensuing trend has been sustained more vigorously in the United States than anywhere else. It reflects an appreciation of the properties of herbs, the post-war cookery renaissance and a new response to the delights of scent in the garden.

Herbs are often untidy plants, and as some of the most important are annuals and biennials, there are almost bound to be gaps in a herb garden at certain times of the year. This is when a formal structure and good permanent features can play a crucial role — in imposing order on a disorderly array of plants and compensating for winter gaps.

Much of the beauty of a herb garden lies in its subtle blend of colours: the greys, greens, blues and yellows of the leaves — which can be variegated, and which also have distinctive shapes. So careful planting is needed, to make the most of contrasts in form and growing season. Herbs need sun, free-draining soil and, except in the warm south where many grow wild, shelter. Like the parterre, a herb garden can be on any scale, from a small arrangement defined by a ground-pattern of low hedges close to the kitchen door, to a much larger more complex scheme which merits a separate garden to itself.

It is crucial, when planning a herb garden, to start by making a firm symmetrical groundplan. Any of the plans given in this book for potagers as well as some for parterres would be suitable for herbs. Take care to hold your picture together by axes related to a central focal point such as a sundial, large pot or a piece of topiary like a pyramid of bay. Additional vistas can be added to focus upon seats, which should always be placed near scented herbs. Do not ignore the possibilities of including, as was done in the past, old-fashioned flowers such as clove pinks and pot marigolds. But do also remember that a herb garden whatever its undoubted delights is not a low-maintenance enterprise.

◀◀ A formal herb garden at its summer apogee shows how quickly the containing boundaries of any scheme can vanish beneath the lush growth. Severe trimming or re-planting will be needed the following winter if the lines of the composition are not to disappear.

◀ This detail of the herb garden designed in 1961 by John Codrington affords a rare instance of a classical formula re-cast in contemporary mode, the pattern being an offspring of the style we now associate with the 1950s.

▼ This tiny herb garden consists of four symmetrical beds bordered with santolina, and a central bed in which rue surrounds a large terracotta crock that gives height to the composition and provides point to a vista.

KITCHEN GARDENS AND POTAGERS

◀ The tradition of the Renaissance potager is still alive in Switzerland. Surrounded by a picket fence, the area is quartered with gravel paths and divided into symmetrical box-edged beds. The small ones, filled with flowers, form a focal point.

▶ The European tradition of the potager reached the USA where it took on a character of its own. Here, at Williamsburg, Virginia, a potager is divided by brick paths with a handsome topiary yew as a centrepiece, with a circle of espaliered fruit trees and a vista to a wooden seat.

The present interest in formal and decorative kitchen gardens or potagers springs from a rediscovery of a European tradition going back to the Renaissance. French country-house gardens are still often divided into two, the parterre and the potager, in exactly the same way as advocated by Charles Etienne and Jean Liébault in their *L'Agriculture et la Maison Rustique* (first edition 1564). They recommended the potager to be enclosed by hedges, walls or an arcaded walk of trellis which would be covered with sweet-smelling jasmine and musk rose, or used as supports for cucumbers or hops. Within, it was laid out in a symmetrical pattern of raised beds. Jacques Boyceau (d. *c.*1633) in his *Traité du Jardinage* (1638) writes of the decorative planting of vegetables: artichokes, for instance, as a border to smaller plants such as strawberries planted as labyrinths. Such an elaborate approach was to reach its apogee in the work of Jean-Baptiste de la Quintinie (1626–88), creator of the *Potager du Roi* at Versailles (1677–83), whose book, *Instructions pour Les Jardins Fruitiers et Potagers* (1690), became a classic reference work. He stated that the only correct shape for a potager was a square, a conclusion reached not only on practical but also on aesthetic grounds.

That book was translated into English in 1693 by John Evelyn (1620–1705), who built on an equally vigorous native tradition. Half a century earlier William Lawson, in his *The Countrie Housewifes Garden* (1617), draws the distinction between the two parts of any garden: though the flower garden must be 'of exquisite forme to the eyes, yet you may not altogether neglect this where your hearbes for the pot doe grow'. This more modest English country-manor-house tradition was to pass to the New World, and is recaptured today in the re-created gardens and orchards of

Williamsburg, Virginia. It is also the one which has been the fount of the present revival of the potager rather than the intimidating and highly labour-intensive kitchen gardens of the great country houses of the eighteenth and nineteenth centuries.

Like a herb garden, a potager demands a firm yet practical groundplan with elements of year-round interest to compensate for the empty beds in winter and the harvesting of crops in summer. Like the herb garden, too, a potager needs shelter to protect the vegetables and establish a microclimate in order to prolong the growing season. This calls for walls, hedges or some form of fencing which can take espaliered fruit trees. Within, you should divide it with paths and place a focal point, such as a pyramid of bay, a sundial, a terracotta pot or even a dwarf fruit tree trained as a dome or goblet, at the centre. You will also probably want to put an arch or a seat at the end of one of the paths. Make a symmetrical pattern of paths, each wide enough to take a wheelbarrow and give easy access for working. You may then build on that geometry in the growing months by the way you plant your vegetables. Spinach, beet, cauliflowers, parsnips, potatoes, onions, French beans and cabbages all look different, so give a thought to their placing apart from the usual consideration of pure practicality, so that there is always a pleasant contrast of shape and colour.

The year-round elements can be edges of the beds in dwarf box, santolina or lavender, and the vertical evergreen features, such as topiary of box or bay pruned to the shape of balls, cones or corkscrews. To these can be added dwarf fruit trees, standard roses and gooseberries and carpenter's work in trellis for runner beans. Remember to place a simple seat in an arbour where you can rest from your substantial labours.

▲ Espaliered fruit trees forming a transparent wall or *claire-voie* give decorative structure to a potager even under snow. A similar screen on a much reduced scale would be an ideal means of dividing a small garden into two, an area near the house for flowers and one further away for vegetables. Fruit trees would succesfully link the two, as they combine spring blossom and autumn produce.

▲ A beautifully espaliered old pear tree in bloom. It would take many years of painstaking but worthwhile pruning to achieve this degree of perfection. Nonetheless, a similar effect can be achieved on a much smaller scale with dwarf rooting fruit stock. If you are lucky enough to have a south-facing wall, an espaliered fruit tree would add an unusual element of great distinction to your garden.

▶ A parade of fruit arches gives a stunning vista to the whole length of the garden. Spring blossom and autumn fruit could only enhance the picture.

This idea would be easily adapted to a much shorter pathway, and could be made into a tunnel by introducing more arches. (These are now available in many prefabricated forms.) A fruit tunnel would be an unusual and productive alternative to a pergola covered in climbers.

▲ This potager demonstrates the importance of vista in planning. Here it is provided by a brick path flanked with lavender and rows of standard gooseberries leading to a box cone and a tunnel beyond.

◀ Even the tiniest potager needs a focal point and height. Here it takes the form of a standard gooseberry.

◀◀ Flowers can provide an axis and focal point to a vegetable garden. A trim circus of box hedging gives on to an avenue of dahlias. The large fruit tree in one bed does not disturb the balance of the composition and the strong, hot colours of the flowers are offset by the fresh greens of the produce.

THE
APPLICATION
OF FORMALITY

The illustrated garden books of the past were conceived as quarries of ideas from which to put together an interesting garden. I can never look at them without some sense of excitement at the hundreds of possibilities they offer for everything from designs for fencing to shapes for rose beds. This book hopes to evoke the same response: to release the reader's own creativity rather than to promote slavish copying of the designs here. No one is going to have exactly the same site as any of the examples which follow, but many may have something similar; and all the designs can be adapted both to differently shaped sites as well as in the way the various elements have been put together. All the way through I have stressed the idea of interchangeability. Nothing is immutable, except, perhaps, existing mature trees that you want to retain, so it is worth while studying all these examples before you make your plan. A garden, after all, is one of the great personal statements which life affords.

The only fixed points in formal garden planning are a few general principles, none of them complicated. They revolve around the basic concepts of geometry and are explained in Chapter One. None of the designs in this book, for obvious reasons, includes a view of the house; yet the house is seminal to all garden planning, for the aim of formal design is to link the one so intimately with the other that they make up a unity of concept. You must start with the architecture of the house on its garden sides and work outwards to create vistas from its windows and entrances.

The style and location of your house, whether in town or country, whether old or new, will also affect the type of garden appropriate to it. Among the designs there are ones for urban as well as country sites, and ideas for gardens in both hot and cold climates and, of course, guidance on how to adapt from one to the other. Often all that needs to be changed is the planting to make it suitable for your climate zone, soil and orientation. The best way to plan a garden is on graph paper, but always remember that if you are marrying various 'rooms' from different designs they must be linked together by vistas.

Three other factors are of importance. The first is commitment. Are you a dedicated gardener or are you looking for ease of maintenance? Be honest about this from the start. Not all of us are destined to be Miss Jekylls. The next is budget. Some formal gardens are relatively inexpensive and many that are more ambitious can be developed in stages over a number of years. But do not stint on them. Untold sums are spent unquestioningly on interior decoration, whereas a Scrooge-like mentality seems suddenly to set in when faced with creating a garden. Finally, there is a question of how long it takes to achieve results. All garden-making is an investment of time, a chunk of one's lifespan. One of the attractions of formal gardens is that, if you can afford the building work, you can have an almost instant result. Planting, it is true, may take ten to fifteen years to reach full maturity. In the past no one objected to that and they lived shorter lives. Neither should we, especially since watching a garden grow and take shape is much of the pleasure.

Two last words: always be guided by your eye in making a garden; always approach it with a sense of joy. Once it becomes a burden it shows in the result. If your garden is a delight to you, that feeling will be communicated to everyone who visits it.

◀ An outward-looking hillside site, terraced on three levels to make three distinctive gardens (see next page).
▲ A treillage arch framing a trough of seasonal plants could be used to terminate a vista in a small urban garden (see page 145).

1. TERRACED GARDEN

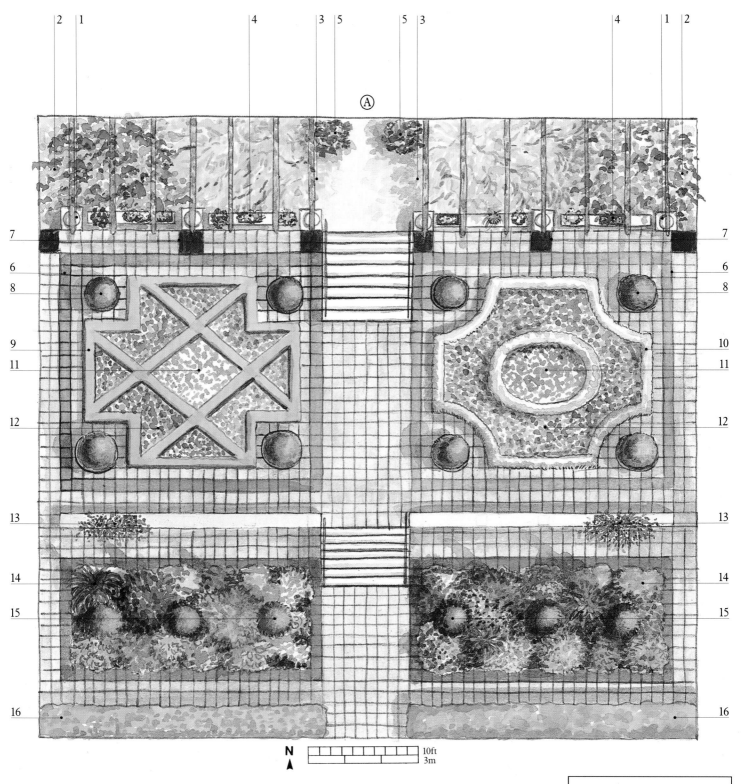

N

10ft
3m

The site is about 60ft (18.2m) wide by 55ft (16.7m) deep with an overall drop of 10ft (3m).

The design is for a site, common enough in warm countries, where a house is built on a southern slope; but the solutions developed here can be applied to any hillside garden. The basic answer is to terrace the sloping area. Here a 10-foot (3-metre) drop from the pergola to the outside road level allows for three separate descending areas to be created; a terrace abutting directly on to the house protected by a pergola, a pair of parterre gardens to look down on, and a final drop to a pair of beds with screening shrubbery.

There is no doubt that this would be an expensive garden to start from scratch. It calls for professional landscaping to construct the retaining walls (taking the problems of drainage into consideration), to lay the paving and build the balustrading. Once established and planted, however, cost would be minimal and its upkeep would require a moderate amount of garden work to replant the parterres for each season (although even these could be planted with groundcover plants), prune the shrubberies and climbing plants and, above all, water all the containers as well as, in dry spells, the beds themselves.

This is an outward-looking garden, since its siting presupposes a view. The pergola creates an outdoor room from which to enjoy the prospect, as well as an area for alfresco eating; it also gives support to some handsome climbing plants which will clothe it with distinction. The design is a classic formal combination of a terrace from which to look down on a parterre below. Like nearly all the features in this garden the parterres — one of box and the other of santolina — give year-long value. Even when devoid of planting in winter, their pattern, reinforced by a symmetrical placing of terracotta pots bearing clipped evergreens and by the geometric paving, is strong enough to sustain interest. A fig tree against the wall beneath the balustrading adds yet another pattern with its carefully trained branches. Descending one more flight of steps, you find two simple beds of screening evergreens to ensure privacy.

I have given four extra designs for the parterres, and any of the six could be used elsewhere. Indeed this entire composition could be just as successful in a virtually flat back garden. In that case you should try to make the pergola terrace just a few steps up from the level of the rest of the garden to give it a little advantage in height over the parterres. Dispense with the second row of balustrading between these and the two shrubbery beds, and close the central vista from the door with a wall fountain.

THE PERGOLA GARDEN

The pergola is made of six reconstituted stone columns (1) with wooden rafters abutting directly on to the house (A). The columns are 9 feet (2.7 metres) in height and support four symmetrically placed climbers planted close to the retaining wall on the level below. The two outer ones are *Vitis* (2) to give leafy shade in summer succeeded in the autumn by crimson and gold foliage. The two flanking the steps are *Wisteria sinensis* (3), to frame the entrance and provide contrasting foliage and beautiful trailing lilac flowers in early summer. Sections of balustrading link the columns and there is space for pots on the coping (4), and on either side of the door (5).

THE PARTERRE GARDEN

Both parterres are inset into paving which emphasizes the geometry (6). On either side against the retaining walls there is a fan-trained brown turkey fig (7), which will ensure handsome summer foliage, autumn fruit and a pretty pattern of branches through the winter. The parterres could be identical; here they are not, but are matched and given height by a large terracotta pot at each corner (8). These are too big to be taken in during the winter and so must be filled with something reasonably robust. Here they have been planted with laurustinus *(Viburnum tinus)* which has small white flowers flushed with pink in winter, kept clipped to form a dome.

One parterre is of dwarf box (9) and the other of lavender cotton (10). Any of the patterns I have suggested below (17, 18, 19 and 20) would work equally well. The colour schemes within could vary from year to year. Each season you should make a plan, beginning with the autumn planting of bulbs for the spring, followed by summer bedding plants, preferably with a long flowering period. Here they are planted with two colours of *Impatiens* (11 and 12).

THE LOWER GARDEN

The retaining wall could have apertures for plants such as aubrieta and *Erigeron mucronatus* that would soften the architecture. Instead, two beds have been made in the paving above (13) for a pair of *Cotoneaster dammeri* trained to cascade downwards. The two flanking beds (14) are for a shrubbery that could be planted with Mediterranean or sub-tropical plants in a warm climate; included here are berberis, hebes, *Senecio greyi, Fatsia japonica,* phormium, cistus and *Cordyline.* It would be lovely to have scented plants flanking the central path to enjoy each time one came in. It is essential that the beds should contain some formal vertical accents to act as sentinels framing the house. Here there are six narrow columnar cypresses (15), but a pair of palm trees either side would be equally effective. The whole is bounded by an evergreen hedge (16) which could be pruned or clipped into a variety of interesting shapes (see page 138).

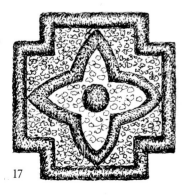

17

18

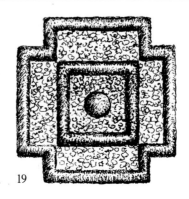

19

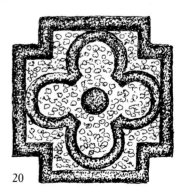

20

2. NEW ENGLAND GEOMETRY

This is a garden inspired by those on the east coast of the United States which keep alive the formal garden tradition of seventeenth-century England in a modest and charming domestic form. This particular design was inspired by a garden in Virginia. The verandah or porch at the back of these houses calls for a patterned garden to be viewed from above, just as parterres always were in the past. This garden was conceived to complement an old weatherboard house or cottage, but it would equally suit one constructed in stone, stucco or brick. It would also sit as easily in a suburban as in a rural setting, and could be made inward-looking by a containing wall or hedge.

This particular type of garden includes a number of specifically American characteristics; the open picket fence, expressing the desire to be outward-looking and unenclosed; the use of gravel paths instead of grass (which is difficult to maintain in parching heat); and the presence of groundcover plants within the parterre to reduce the workload. But perhaps the most interesting feature is the absence of sculpture — proof that it is perfectly possible for a formal garden to succeed without the feature often mistakenly thought to be fundamental.

The absence of statuary is made good by an ambitious topiary focal point. If you opt for my choice of silver-edged holly, it will take at least ten years to complete. By the fifth year, however, the intent will be more than evident and the insertion of a cane the height you wish it to reach will make the project even clearer to any doubting visitor.

Another attractive feature of American formal gardens is their informality! The edging to the beds is loosely trimmed so that it seems to meander around the precise shape of a bed rather than tightly contain it in rigid lines. The sense of informality is increased by the trees which soar upwards from the beds and the shrubs which tumble over on to the paths. These I have suggested should be gravel, which is very much in keeping with the informality and is not costly. They could, of course, be paved, but take care to make the paving interesting by using a mixture of materials and creating patterns at some of the crossings, in particular that at the centre.

This is formality with no delusions of grandeur. It is a style which deserves to be re-exported back across the Atlantic, as it accords perfectly with today's demand for small-scale gardens with maximum style and medium maintenance. Although the length of time required to achieve the focal point might seem daunting, the remainder of the garden would be fully mature within a few years. It is also an inexpensive garden, for a seat could easily be substituted for the summerhouse.

The alternative design (*far right below*) calls for the same treatment and both are patterns which would be suitable for a rose garden or a herb garden. In a rose garden the planting of the outer beds should remain the same and the inner ones should be planted in blocks of not more than two colours of roses, with standards to add height in the absence of the trees. For the herb garden, formal elements in box and bay would be necessary, and in both cases I would replace the central topiary holly with a permanent feature.

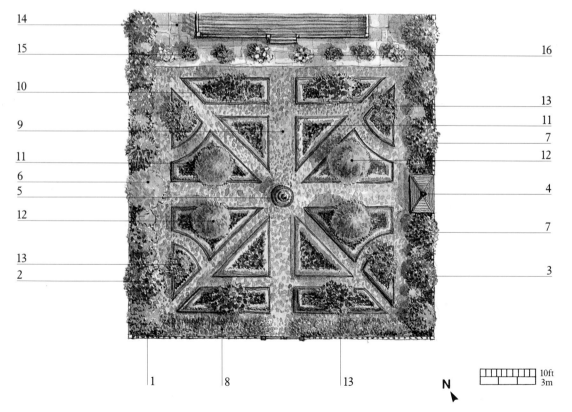

14
15
10
9
11
6
5
12
13
2

16
13
11
7
12

4

7

3

1   8   13

N

10ft
3m

THE GARDEN

The garden is surrounded on three sides by a picket fence (**1**). On two sides there are shrubberies (**2** and **3**), containing evergreens inter-mingled with deciduous shrubs including *Viburnum opulus*, *V. davidii*, *Daphne mezereum*, *Ceanothus* 'Autumnal Blue', *Skimmia japonica*, *Hibiscus syriacus*, *Choisya ternata* and *Cornus alba*. In the middle of the south-west shrubbery there is a gazebo (**4**) sited for shade but also on the main axis in order to view the topiary centrepiece (**5**) and, in the shrub border opposite, an interesting small tree (**6**), perhaps a *Prunus sargentii* for its early autumn colour. Either side of the gazebo are two sweet-smelling *Philadelphus* (**7**). Along the picket fence with the front gate there is a planting of spring bulbs which have been replaced with feathery lavender-blue catmint (*Nepeta*) (**8**) in the summer.

The garden is divided by gravel walks (**9**). Its focal point (**5**) is a

The site is about 55ft (16.9m) square.

handsome silver-leafed holly (*Ilex aquifolium* 'Silver Queen') clipped into tiers with a ball at the top. This will grow slowly to a height of about 8 feet (2.4 metres). Yew (*Taxus baccata*) would grow faster but the foliage is less interesting. For those in a hurry, golden privet (*Ligustrum ovalifolium* 'Aureomarginatum') is an option, although this will never give more than a very loose sculptural shape. If you are short of patience a piece of statuary will give instant effect, but it will erode the essential simplicity of the garden.

The beds are edged (**10**) with dwarf lavender cotton (*Santolina chamaecyparissus corsica*), which will require clipping at least once a season and replacing with cuttings every five to eight years. You could as easily use dwarf box (*Buxus sempervirens* 'Suffruticosa') or germander (*Teucrium*). The eight inner beds (**11**) are filled with pretty groundcover, a form of the periwinkle *Vinca minor* which has blue flowers in early summer; and

they are given height by four small trees (**12**), ornamental thorns such as *Crataegus × lavallei* or *C. prunifolia*, kept pruned as mopheads. These would provide spring blossom and brilliant autumn fruits that persist on the branches well into winter.

The eight outlying beds (**13**) are planted with rugosa roses, resilient disease-resistant shrubs which only require shaping in late winter. The colours have been

chosen to harmonize with the others in the garden: pink *Rosa* 'Frau Dagmar Hastrup' and crimson-purple *R.* 'Roseraie de l'Hay'. Beneath there would be room for a carpet of pansies. The terrace (**14**) outside the house (**A**) provides space for containers with summer plantings. I would favour purple petunias (**15**) and white hydrangeas (**16**). Standard fuchsias would also strike a more than spectacular note.

ALTERNATIVE PLAN

This simple alternative ground-plan would accommodate the same planting scheme; but I would double the number of mophead trees to maintain the symmetry of the pattern.

3. FAMILY AND SECRET GARDEN

The division of a garden into two distinct and contrasting areas is one of the great opportunities offered by formal planning. In this garden it enables us to combine a large open family space, including a substantial area of grass and a summerhouse, with a secret, elegant parterre garden. It is a division which very usefully establishes 'go' and 'no go' areas for those enemies to horticulture, children. A generous terrace running the whole width of the house together with a large circular lawn provide ample space for everything from bicycle racing to ball games. The Secret Garden should be ruled 'out of bounds'. Both gardens are inward-looking, and a substantial dividing hedge is essential. Yew, which will take about ten years to mature, is the ideal plant. Other, modern varieties of conifer will give quicker results but the effect will fall short of the deep green density of the yew.

The Family Garden is geometric but fairly informal in its planting, with mixed herbaceous plants in soft colours in the spandrels of the lawn to tumble over and break its edges. Four fastigiate columnar evergreens in the corners give height to the borders; and the entrances to the lawn should be emphasized by a symmetrical planting. The sunken siting of the lawn is an advantage though not essential; but if you contrive at least one step down, you will be surprised how much it enhances the composition.

The Secret Garden is conceived as a place of quiet harmony achieved by its sense of enclosure and the restful stately geometry of the patterns of the beds. Patterns for such parterres, or knots as they are usually known, are virtually endless (see pages 32–4 and 104–5). They provide year-round pleasure and can be enlivened in spring by bulbs and in summer by annuals planted in blocks of colour.

The entire garden is enclosed by a substantial shrubbery — mainly evergreen to ensure privacy and to conceal any unattractive fencing, but partly deciduous to add blossom, fruit and colourful autumn foliage.

The garden is strong on vistas: from the house to the summerhouse, from the terrace to the statue, and from the seat in the Secret Garden to the little wall fountain in the Family Garden. It is the vistas which, more than any other feature, hold these two gardens together, but special thought must also be given to the views back towards the house.

The built elements are major and costly; but many are optional or can be simplified. The obelisks in the Secret Garden could be dispensed with; if you do this then square off the box hedging, re-adjust the inner pattern and substitute an upright cone for the ball at the centre to give the beds height. The balustrading along the terrace is also not essential, or could be added later. But the Family Garden does call for a pair of sentinels, perhaps urns, at the terrace entrance. Although the ambitious paving scheme can be simplified, a reduction to slabs *en masse* would render it municipal. If the problem is finance, stagger the construction. Plant the dividing hedge first, then the Family Garden, and only begin the Secret Garden when you are ready.

Both gardens call for medium rather than intensive maintenance. Either could stand as a garden in its own right; the Secret Garden, for instance, would (with modifications) make a splendid small town garden; and either composition would sit happily in the suburbs or the country.

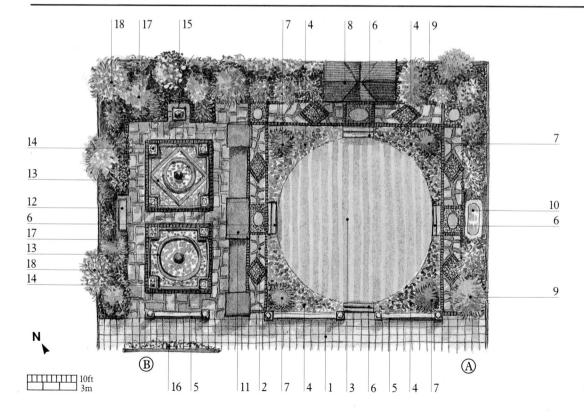

THE FAMILY GARDEN
Outside the house (**A**), a paved terrace (**1**) leads on to a path (**2**) of stone with brick edging and pebbled details. It encloses a circular lawn (**3**) with beds (**4**) in the spandrels. The terrace is handsomely bounded by balustrading (**5**) and entrance to the lawn is by a small flight of steps (**6**) on each of the four sides. The planting within the beds (**4**) could be herbaceous with a spring planting of tulips and *Myosotis*, but could equally be a mixture of roses and grey foliage plants. In the four corners there are fastigiate evergreens, Irish yew (*Taxus baccata* 'Fastigiata') (**7**), though you could use one of the more interesting columnar conifers such as *Juniperus virginiana* 'Skyrocket' or *Chamaecyparis lawsoniana* 'Columnaris Glauca'. At the far end is a summerhouse (**8**). Two sides are filled with shrubs and climbers (**9**) including

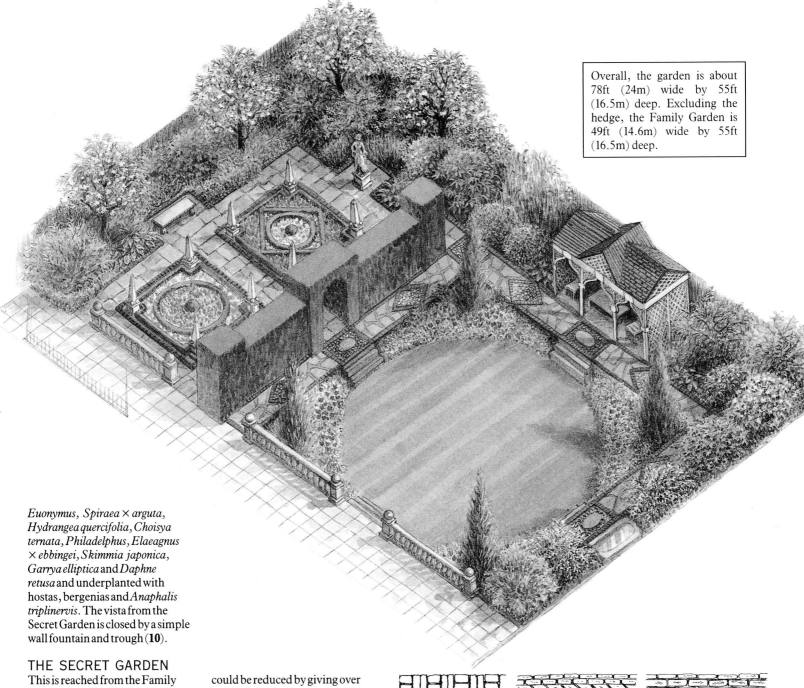

Overall, the garden is about 78ft (24m) wide by 55ft (16.5m) deep. Excluding the hedge, the Family Garden is 49ft (14.6m) wide by 55ft (16.5m) deep.

Euonymus, Spiraea × arguta, Hydrangea quercifolia, Choisya ternata, Philadelphus, Elaeagnus × ebbingei, Skimmia japonica, Garrya elliptica and *Daphne retusa* and underplanted with hostas, bergenias and *Anaphalis triplinervis*. The vista from the Secret Garden is closed by a simple wall fountain and trough (**10**).

THE SECRET GARDEN

This is reached from the Family Garden by way of an arch in a thick yew hedge (**11**). A seat or bench is placed on the axis (**12**) and mid-way between the two parterres (**13**) which are of dwarf box (*Buxus sempervirens* 'Suffruticosa') and have reconstituted stone obelisks (**14**) at the corners. Both parterres (**3** and **4**) can be subject to changing annual displays; here, in the spring, segments have white or pink tulips. This could be succeeded in the summer by mignonette and calendulas. Work

could be reduced by giving over some of each knot to a more or less permanent planting of clipped santolina or purple sage, for instance.

The vista from the terrace is closed by a statue (**15**), and the view the other way is screened by trellis in front of the garage (**B**) with climbing plants (**16**). The two sides (**17**) are planted with shrubs, and with two pairs of crab apple trees (**18**) (*Malus* 'John Downie') to give height, blossom and beautiful fruit.

ALTERNATIVE PATHS

Pattern within paths and paving is open to variation both in choice of materials and in the ways they can be laid. Brick is especially useful as it is available in so many colours — which can be teamed to the

architecture of your house — and can be laid in so many different patterns. Here are three variants which would give pattern and permanent interest to any garden. Two are of brick and one of brick and pebbles set in concrete.

4. PERGOLA GARDEN

A straight rectangle that juts out from the back of a town or suburban terrace or semi-detached house is an extremely common shape of garden which, by its very location, demands to be inward-looking. Such a garden can easily be boring unless the area is divided, giving a sense that there is more space than there really is, and an element of mystery added. One way of achieving all this is to use a pergola to divide the garden and flank it with contrasting 'rooms'.

The pergola is also a handsome architectural feature in its own right for the display of a range of climbers and a pleasant shady place in which to sit on a sunny day. In hot climates shade will be a prime consideration but in cooler climates pergolas are often better when only lightly clothed with climbers. With skill a toolshed can be concealed within. Also if the central support posts are widely spaced, the pergola can be made to frame the main vista of the garden.

A pergola can serve as a bridgehead dividing many sorts of garden compartments one from another. Here the contrast is between a formal paved garden of herbs and herbaceous plants, and a tranquil area of lawn, which is enclosed by an evergreen hedge. A pleasant succession of moods is thus created. Initially comes the paved court inset with beds, a handsome sundial bearing a gilded sphere and a plethora of herbs and flowers. Then follows the pergola, which provides ample space to indulge in a whole range of climbing plants. And finally there is a cool green enclosure which can be elaborated upon or not according to resources. The paving, the pergola and the ornaments are all quite costly, so that in this part of the garden you may decide to opt for the simple crenellated version of the hedge and to choose a single large urn as the garden's focal point. To have an accent here is essential. If cost is a problem it should take precedence even over the sundial, which could be replaced by a large well-planted crock.

Overall, this design calls for a moderate amount of work from the gardener. The design for the little formal garden would do as well for a rose garden and its place here next to the house could easily be taken by virtually any of the other parterre designs, particularly those on pages 128–9.

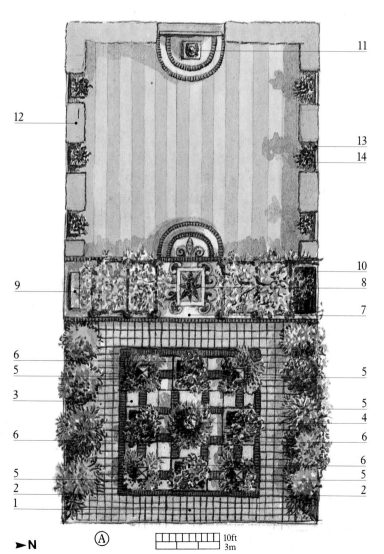

►N   Ⓐ   10ft / 3m

THE HERB AND HERBACEOUS GARDEN

Outside the house (**A**) is a terrace (**1**) with two flanking borders of mainly evergreen shrubs (**2**) which include *Fatsia japonica, Choisya ternata, Deutzia* species, *Mahonia, Syringa* species, *Camellia × williamsii* 'Donation', *Spiraea × arguta, Paeonia lutea* var. *ludlowii, Daphne × burkwoodii* and *Viburnum opulus*. Both are underplanted with various shade-tolerant plants. The middle of the garden is paved in an interesting chequerboard of stone slabs and brick (**3**). Its focal point is a sundial with a gilded sphere on top (**4**). If something else is substituted for this, make sure it does not duplicate or obscure the garden's main focal point at the far end of the vista (**11**). Five beds (**5**) are given to herbs: the central one has rosemary around the sundial; the other four have a box pyramid for height surrounded in the main by culinary herbs. The four beds with hedges of dwarf box (**6**) are filled with a mixture of seasonal plantings and perennials.

THE PERGOLA

The pergola, constructed of brick pillars and wooden beams, is on a raised base (**7**) of crazy paving offset by a formal containing edge of brick and a decorative patterned centrepiece (**8**) leading out towards the steps to the lawn. Care must be taken to leave spaces near the pillars for planting climbers. The construction itself is of wood. Planting will depend on the orientation of your pergola and should take account of contrasting foliage and bloom over a long season. This pergola faces east and west, making it suitable for many plants, including those that are self-supporting and those that need to be tied in. Here it is planted with *Wisteria sinensis*. At the southern end there is a seat (**9**) and, at the northern end, a toolshed (**10**) has been concealed.

THE LAWN GARDEN

This garden is a simple lawn enclosed by a hedge with a major focal point – a statue – in the centre at the far end (**11**). The hedge (**12**) is of a firethorn (*Pyracantha rogersiana*) which should be pruned to shape in spring and summer. It will take about ten years to achieve the arcading but the result will be magnificent, with white flowers in summer followed by orange-red berries in the autumn. The arches are backed by trellis (**13**) painted white and each of them contains an urn (**14**) which bears a seasonal planting.

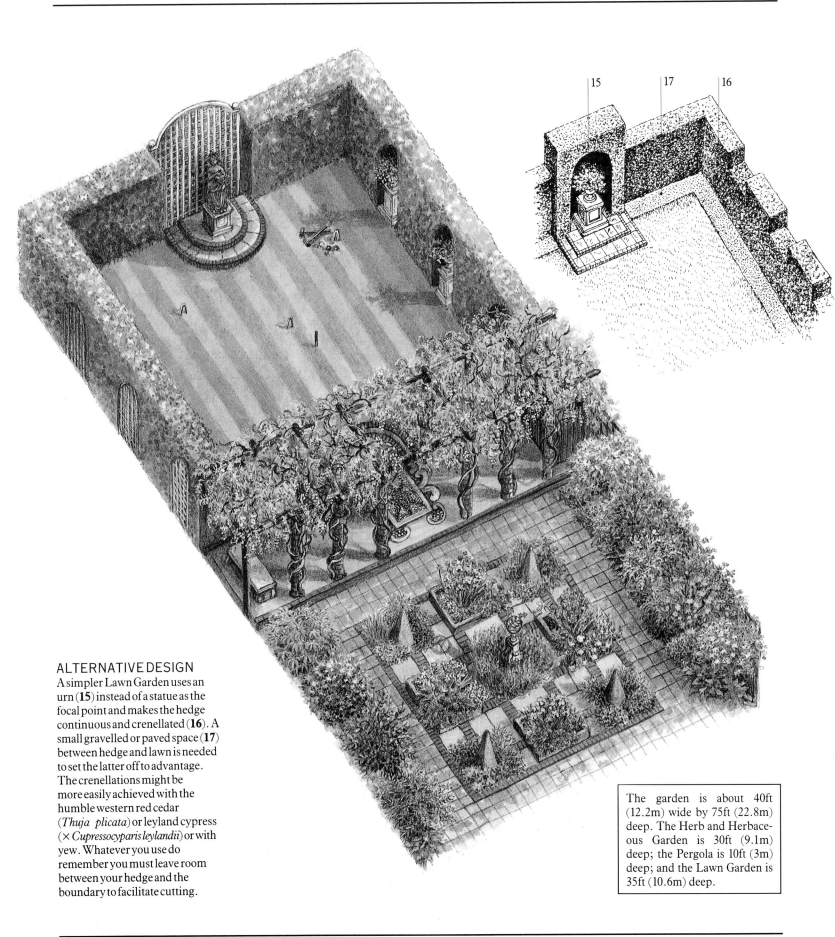

ALTERNATIVE DESIGN

A simpler Lawn Garden uses an urn (**15**) instead of a statue as the focal point and makes the hedge continuous and crenellated (**16**). A small gravelled or paved space (**17**) between hedge and lawn is needed to set the latter off to advantage. The crenellations might be more easily achieved with the humble western red cedar (*Thuja plicata*) or leyland cypress (× *Cupressocyparis leylandii*) or with yew. Whatever you use do remember you must leave room between your hedge and the boundary to facilitate cutting.

The garden is about 40ft (12.2m) wide by 75ft (22.8m) deep. The Herb and Herbaceous Garden is 30ft (9.1m) deep; the Pergola is 10ft (3m) deep; and the Lawn Garden is 35ft (10.6m) deep.

5. LAWN AND VISTA GARDEN

This is an inward-looking formal garden which plays a spectacular optical trick to give the visitor the illusion that there is far more to the garden than is really the case. The device is the very simple one of creating a peepshow which carries the perspective of one garden right through the heart of a second — in this instance a concealed working kitchen garden. Close-cut grass, flanked by an avenue of fruit trees, leads up to an urn on a pedestal encompassed by a semi-circle of clipped yew. Some kind of focal point is essential for this vista but it could as equally be a bust on a column, a statue, or an obelisk. The two fastigiate trees in the distance add to the deception. In spring the scene would be one of nodding blossom in an allée of naturalized daffodils or narcissi. In autumn there would be the rosy glow of the fruit on the trees.

Here the concealed area is a down-to-earth kitchen garden, toolshed and compost heap. A similar treatment could conceal any basic or downright ugly service area such as a garage, workshop or even a children's play space. You could develop it into a fully fledged potager along the lines of that in Garden 6 (pages 114–5) or garden 9 (pages 124-5). If produce is not required, another successful solution would be the same treatment as in the Wild Garden in Garden 6. The path in the Vista Garden could be a continuation of the brick path in the Lawn Garden with the urn set one step up on a paved platform. The illusion of distance will be increased if the path rises by steps, however slight, at intervals, and even more if it is made to narrow slightly as it converges on the urn.

The Lawn Garden is very simple: the only elements requiring intensive maintenance are the pair of herbaceous borders near the house, and even these are optional. They could easily be replaced by shrubbery, as on the two other sides. Otherwise the garden consists of nothing more than lawn, dissecting paths, and four flowering trees. When the planting is as simple as this, enrichment must go into some of the built features. In particular the path must be interesting to look at in contrast to the plain flanking turf. Here a mixture of patterned brick with cobbles or setts at the crossings is suggested but there are endless variations. To provide further interest I have suggested, as the Lawn Garden's focal point, a sundial topped by a gilded sphere to catch the light.

If you dispense with the herbaceous borders and potager, this is a fairly low-maintenance garden requiring seasonal mowing of the lawn, annual pruning of the shrubs, flowering trees and hedges, and weed-killing the paths. The heaviest capital outlay would be on the paths and the two ornaments. The general effect of the garden would be there from the initial planting, but its chief feature, the surprise vista of yew, would have to wait ten or more years for its full realization. You could plant a faster growing evergreen hedge but it would be well worth waiting for the yew. This garden would be as appropriate for the suburbs as for the country, and the Lawn Garden is a valid design for a garden on its own.

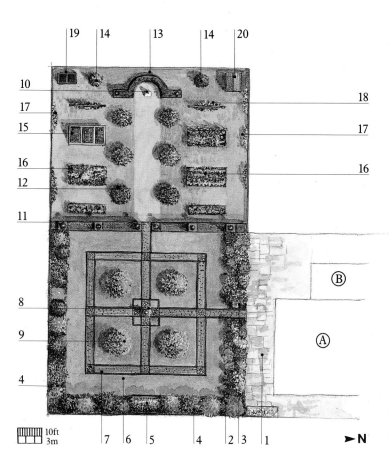

10ft
3m

► N

THE LAWN GARDEN

Outside the house (**A**) and garage (**B**) is a paved terrace (**1**). A path bisects an herbaceous border (**2**), with containers (**3**) for seasonal plantings flanking the entrance. Beds (**4**) on either side of the garden are planted with a preponderance of evergreen shrubs and specimen conifers to conceal the fencing and ensure privacy. On the east side there is a garden seat (**5**) placed so as to enjoy the vista and the evening sun. Over it there is a simple pergola arch for roses and sweet-smelling climbers. The lawn (**6**) is quartered by brick paths (**7**) with cobbles set into concrete at the crossings and corners, and has a sundial (**8**) at the centre. The choice of the four trees (**9**) is important: they should achieve interest for most of the year. I suggest a crab apple *(Malus)* such as *M.* 'Golden Hornet' or *M.* 'Red Sentinel', which would give spring flowering and brilliant autumn fruits, or *Amelanchier lamarckii* for white spring flowers and glowing autumn tints.

THE VISTA GARDEN

The vista to an urn (**10**) is seen through a scalloped yew hedge (**11**). The close-cut grass walk is flanked by a small avenue of fruit trees (**12**) on dwarfing rootstocks, underplanted with bulbs. The urn is backed by a semi-circle of yew (**13**). The structural hedges could be western red cedar, beech, hornbeam or even privet instead of yew, any of which would be far less effective but grow much faster. The formal planting is completed by a pair of upright trees (**14**), my preference being for 'Dawyck' beech *(Fagus sylvatica* 'Fastigiata'). On either side of the avenue there is the kitchen garden with a cage for soft fruit (**15**) and beds (**16**) for salad stuff and cut flowers, rhubarb, Jerusalem artichokes and other vegetables and herbs, all subject to rotation. The north- and south-facing fences have room to train fruit trees, acid cherries on the north and apple or peach trees on the south (**17**). Trellis screens (**18**) with roses or vines conceal the compost heap (**19**) and toolshed (**20**).

Overall, the site is about 85ft (25.9m) wide and 140ft (42.6m) deep. The Lawn Garden is about 72ft (21.9m) deep and the Vista Garden about 64ft (19.5m) deep.

ALTERNATIVE PLAN
An alternative plan for the Lawn Garden replaces the pattern of rectangular paths with a diamond and re-sites the four trees into the spandrels. A further enhancement would be the introduction of a flowerbed around the central sundial.

Both lay-outs would be suitable for other types of formal garden. The quarters of grass could equally be four rose or herb beds edged with lavender. Height, however, would need to be added by means of standard roses or box cones to compensate for the loss of the trees.

6. POND GARDEN AND POTAGER

This is the most complicated of all the designs given in this book. It includes water, a lawn flanked by yew buttresses, a wild compartment and a potager. Yet the overall size of the garden is surprisingly small. It shows that by creating a series of 'rooms' it is possible to incorporate many more disparate elements than could successfully be handled in one open space. The size of the garden compartments must bear some relation to the size of the house — the larger the house, the larger the garden rooms should be. A sensible approach to this type of arrangement would be to regard it as four separate gardens linked by vistas, and indeed any of the compartments could be made to form the basis of a complete garden.

This is an expensive garden calling for a professional builder's work on the paving, change of level, pond and summerhouse. Because the built features give the garden its very strong identity and because most are required from the outset, constructing the garden in phases would not be easy. This is therefore a garden that demands a heavy initial commitment of both money and work.

It is also a garden of tremendous contrasts, which makes it especially attractive. The vista from the seat by the little pond would be striking at all times of the year, as you look across the water reflecting the sky and over the greensward with the yew buttresses receding into the distance to the statue silhouetted against the shrubbery. Walking up the main garden path in order to harvest produce in the Potager would always be a delight; so would sitting in the gazebo looking through the four box-edged beds with their small fruit trees bearing blossom in spring and fruit in autumn. Then there is a view from the comfortable trellis arbour along the path leading through to the Wild Garden with its rough-cut grass, spring bulbs and summer display of rugosa roses. This area elicits further delights, for it contains a little avenue of mophead acacias leading to an urn, best viewed from the house or terrace across the pond. It is important to consider the views from the opposite direction, too; you may need to plant climbers against the house or to place pairs of containers either with architecturally interesting plants or with profuse seasonal planting beside doors or French windows.

Given the garden's scale and detail, the on-going workload is surprisingly not heavy. The garden near the house only requires seasonal mowing, annual clipping of the hedge and pruning of the shrubberies. The flowerbed around the statue alone signals a more sustained attention. The Wild Garden calls for pruning the mopheads and rough-cutting the grass. But the Potager does require regular attention. No one should embark on this unless really interested or with the prospect of having additional labour. But with alterations it is a design which could become, for instance, a rose garden. Certainly it would be a perfect position for a rose garden, or for a turf and topiary garden (see pages 36–9).

The variants on this garden are almost limitless. On page 116 I give just one re-arrangement of the same elements, but you could combine any number of the other ideas in this book, such as a parterre and pergola in place of the pond. The scope and possibilities should be a tremendous stimulus to anyone who wishes to create an equally ambitious composition of their own.

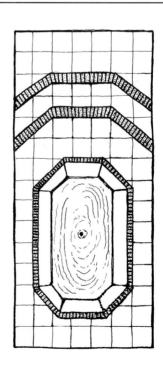

ALTERNATIVE PONDS AND STEPS

The four alternative designs given here are intended for a pond and steps as they occur in this garden, but they can be adapted for other sites and enlarged or altered to fit with mirror-image steps. They use stone or imitation stone together with brick. A strong geometric shape is essential for the formal display of water—like a mirror in a frame. As you look down on water, the surround to it should be interesting but not assertive as it is a feature that will be continually noticed. Square, rectangular or circular shapes are, of course, also classic solutions to the display of water.

The garden, including the paved terrace at the back of the house, is about 80ft (24.4m) wide by 70ft (21.3m) deep. The Lawn Garden is about 57ft (17.5m) wide by 31ft (9.4m) deep. The Pond Garden is about 25ft (7.6m) wide by 35ft (10.8m) deep. The Wild Garden is about 33ft (10m) wide by 28ft (11.1m) deep. The Potager is about 50ft (15.2m) wide by 34ft (10.4m) deep.

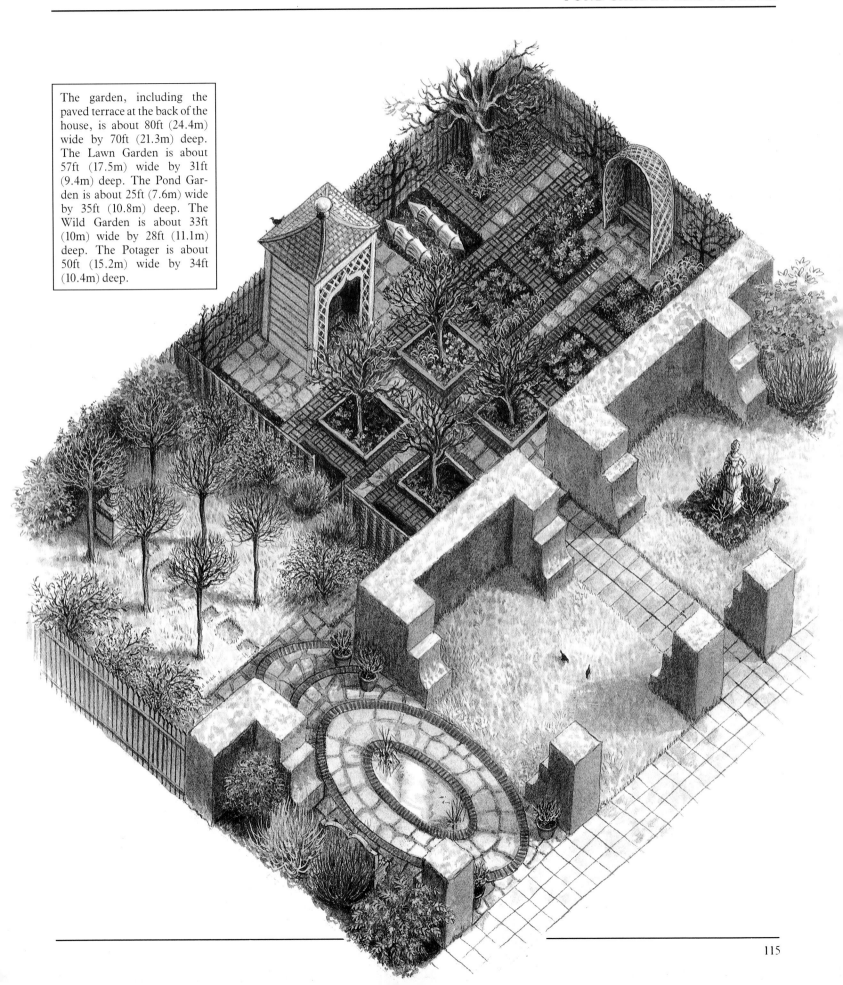

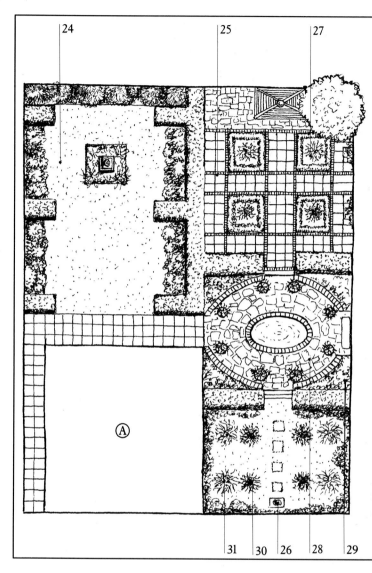

24 25 27

31 30 26 28 29

Ⓐ

ALTERNATIVE PLAN

The plan above contains all the features of the original design but they have been rearranged for a different, smaller, L-shaped site. It shows how you can move around and combine elements of any of the designs in this book in different ways. Here the Lawn Garden (**24**) is reversed so that the buttress vista is seen from the house (**A**). The Potager (**25**) is much smaller and a completely different vista results, with the urn of the Wild Garden (**26**) facing the Gothick gazebo across the pond. In the Potager the apple trees are replaced by four standard roses (**27**). The Pond Garden (**28**) becomes a sunken enclosure with hedges on two sides, offering the chance to grow silver-grey foliage plants in the spandrels (**29**). In the Wild Garden, as there is no space for an avenue, a symmetrical planting of four flowering trees (**30**) and rugosa roses (**31**) might be apposite.

alternative would be to introduce a single fountain jet. However shallow they are, it is vital to remember that ponds are a hazard to children. Large terracotta pots (**9**) with hydrangeas give added interest to the area.

THE WILD GARDEN

The vista is backed by evergreen shrubs and climbers (**10**) to set off an ornament (**11**) to advantage. The area has rough-cut grass crossed by large stepping stones to allow for a naturalized planting of narcissi in the spring. The tiny avenue is of a variety of the false acacia (*Robinia pseudoacacia* 'Inermis') (**12**) kept trimmed to mopheads. Another treatment would be to formalize the space a little more by making an avenue of standard roses, which would require beds, but that would call for the grass to be regularly mown. If you opt for roses keep the colours pale. On either side I suggest planting rugosa roses (**13**) which are vigorous and resilient, highly scented and require little attention. A pair of rosemary bushes (**14**) act as sentinels to the potager.

THE POTAGER

Paved with slabs (**15**) edged with brick, the potager is focussed upon four beds edged with dwarf box (**16**). In the centre of each is an apple tree (**17**) on a dwarfing rootstock (M9). As it would be difficult to grow vegetables in their shade I would suggest a formal underplanting of *Anaphalis triplinervis* or *Lamium maculatum* 'Beacon Silver' (**18**). The south-west facing fence (**19**) is ideal for espaliered fruit trees, while the north-west fence might support acid cherries (**20**), with space in front for salad and culinary herbs. The woven fencing (**21**) could support runner beans; other beds (**22**) can be used for crop rotation, including winter vegetables, while polythene tunnels (**23**) protect winter salad.

THE TERRACE

The terrace (**1**) runs the whole width of the back of the house (**A**). The garage (**B**) and side entrance (**C**) are screened by trellis (**2**) with climbing plants. When siting the yew buttresses (**3**) take care that they do not coincide with a window or door; their somewhat austere appearance from the terrace side could be ameliorated by placing a series of finials in front of them, for example a ball or a pineapple on a plinth.

THE LAWN GARDEN

The most distinctive feature is the yew hedge with its massive buttresses (**3**). These will eventually provide a great sense of theatre and spectacle but will take at least ten years to reach a mature state. The shapes can be varied; you could, for instance, add a finial or a ball at the top. The planting of the flowerbed (**4**) around the statue (**5**) can be something as simple as *Nepeta* or *Stachys lanata*, or combined with low-growing roses, but if you wish to add more year-round colour you could have a spring planting of crocus then tulips, followed by a summer one of annuals, such as petunias, and finally winter-flowering pansies. It would also be possible to introduce herbaceous borders between the buttresses. At the far end there is a simple border (**6**) chiefly of evergreens but with a few deciduous shrubs for autumn or winter colour.

THE POND GARDEN

A predominantly evergreen screening border (**7**) matches that at the end of the Lawn Garden (**6**). To prevent leaves sinking into the water during the autumn, stretch some black netting across its surface. The pond (**8**) is there chiefly for its reflective qualities, but its surface could be enlivened by a few water plants. An

10

13

21

9

3

7

8

3

2

11 12 13 14 22 15 17 18 16 19

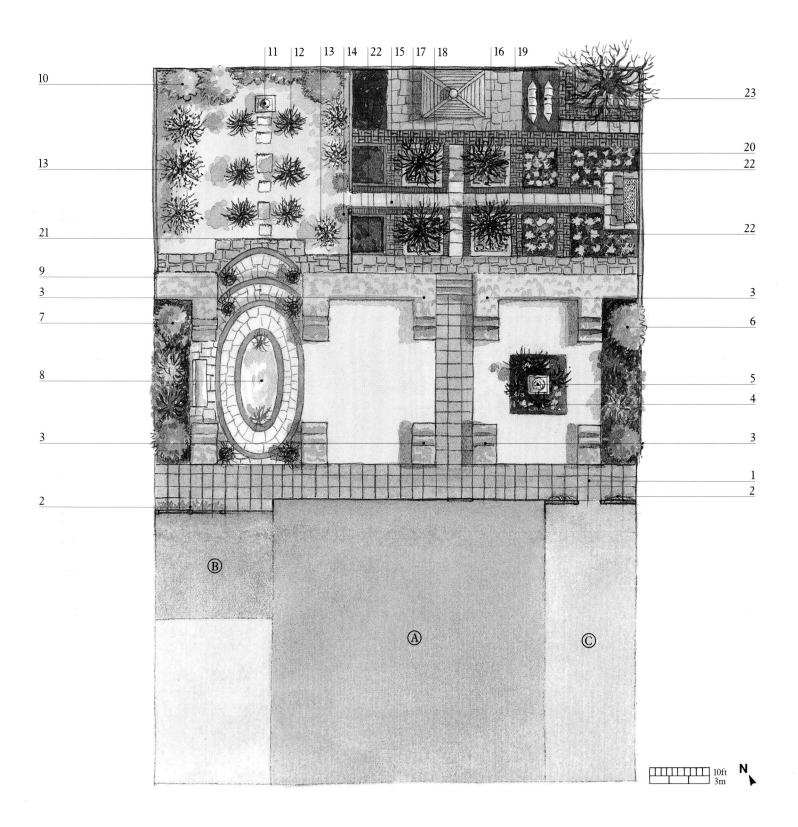

23

20
22

22

3

6

5
4

3

1
2

Ⓑ

Ⓐ

Ⓒ

10ft
3m

N

7. COUNTRY ROSE GARDEN AND POTAGER

Even the most irregular and awkward sites can be formalized: it means imposing geometry on the groundplan, laying paving and planting hedges to create formal enclosures. But consider carefully the preservation of any existing mature trees and hedges and see how they can be integrated into the new scheme. In this triangular site there was a splendid old tree in one corner which allowed for the creation of a small ecological garden of wild flowers and grasses, a perfect foil to the Rose Garden which it adjoins. The existing hedge of hawthorn has been left in all but two places. Remember it, too, can be trained, for example by cutting the top into patterns, or by allowing standards to form.

The only position large enough to take a Rose Garden was away from the house and hidden from all the windows except for those on the first floor on the north side, but this is no disadvantage for few things in garden design give a greater *frisson* of delight than the discovery of secret enclosures. The site also allows for a decorative Potager close to the back of the house. With regular tending this should give as much interest to the owner as the Rose Garden. The octagon, quartered by narrow brick paths, has an evergreen focal point, a bay tree trained as a pyramid, and the four beds have standard roses to add height. An edging of dwarf box would make a pretty addition.

One of the attractions of formalizing an irregular space is that it brings emphasis to any areas which cannot be included in the formal scheme. In this case it not only permits the creation of a little Wild Garden, but in the odd space between the Potager and Rose Garden two fruit trees could be put in, with a generous underplanting of interesting shrubs and groundcover plants to create a long flowering season.

Since the Rose Garden and Potager call for considerable commitment, the area in front of the house should be organized for easy maintenance. Fastigiate yews act as sentinels to the entrance path; there is space for climbers up the front of the house and small beds for shrubs and perennials along the front fence.

Having so many separate areas means that the garden is never without interest at any time of the year. Although both the Rose Garden and the Potager are at their best in summer, other parts will be rewarding in spring, with bulbs pushing up through the grass and hellebores in bloom, or in the autumn, when there will be the fruit on the trees. This is not an expensive garden and its creation could be phased over several years. The important thing to do first is plant the hedges; everything else will be fully mature within five years.

The designs for both the Rose Garden and the Potager can easily be adapted for other purposes—herbs and flowers, certainly. If the Rose Garden design is used for flowers, remember to preserve the pattern through the planting and the colour within the beds and perhaps to add small decorative trees in place of the rose obelisks.

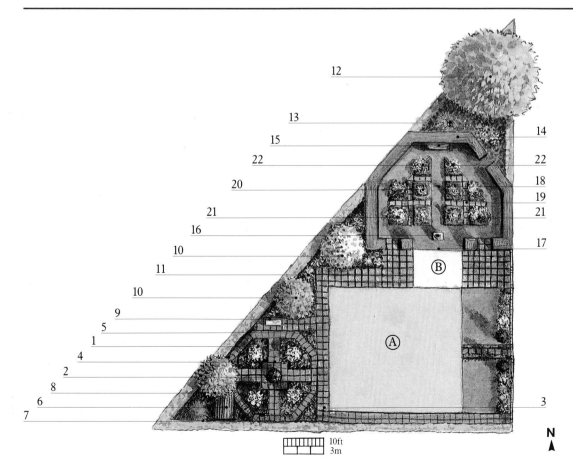

10ft
3m

N

THE POTAGER

There are four beds (**1**) for the rotation of crops, each with a standard *Rosa* 'Iceberg'. At the centre (**2**) there is an obelisk of bay but a large terracotta pot or yew topiary would be equally appropriate. The main paths (**3**) are of slabs and the paths which cross the beds (**4**) might be of dark-coloured brick. The spandrels (**5**) near the house could contain culinary herbs. A toolstore clothed with evergreen climbers (**6**) conceals the compost heap (**7**) while a *Sorbus* (**8**) closes the vista with spring flowers and autumn berries. A wooden seat (**9**) asks to be surrounded by shrubs with sweet-smelling flowers.

THE LINKING AREA

Two fruit trees (**10**) (for example, compatible varieties of apple to allow cross-pollination) add height to this space, which has an informal planting of shade-tolerant small shrubs and groundcover plants such as hostas, geraniums, pulmonarias and hellebores. A container (**11**) anchors the vista of the paths around the house (**A**) in both directions.

THE WILD GARDEN
Rough-cut grass under the mature oak tree (**12**) has a naturalized planting of wild flowers — primroses, cowslips — with a sprinkling of spring bulbs (**13**) and a *Viburnum davidii*.

THE ROSE GARDEN
The garden is enclosed by an 8-foot-(2.7-metre)-high yew hedge (**14**) to act as a foil to the complex scene within.

The main axis is north–south, with a vista from a seat on a paved area (**15**) to a statue (**16**) silhouetted against the wall of the garage (**B**) which is disguised by painted trellis smothered in climbing roses (**17**). The focal point provided by the statue is essential to the garden, although you could substitute an urn which could take a winter planting of pansies. Grass walks (**18**) surround and bisect the ten rose beds, which are themselves divided by paving (**19**) into two groups. All are edged with dwarf lavender. The four central square beds (**20**) have painted wooden obelisks at the centre for height, which call for a climber such as the scented rose-pink repeat-flowering *Rosa* 'Aloha'. Of the six surrounding beds, two (**21**) are large enough to take the snowy white rugosa *R.* 'Blanc Double de Coubert', while the smaller beds (**22**) might have the floribunda *R.* 'Saratoga'. The Rose Garden would then be a symphony of pink and white, grey and blue, against a backcloth of greensward and yew. Alternative colour schemes are of course possible: yellow and white for instance. The inclusion of hip-bearing roses, such as some of the rugosas, in a couple of the larger beds will give added interest in autumn. Do remember that colour control is absolutely crucial. Keep the colours soft and avoid the virulent hues which would disturb the tranquillity.

The site is triangular with two sides of about 90ft (27m) and 100ft (30m,), and a third side of about 135ft (41.1m).

ALTERNATIVE DESIGN
A yew hedge and circular grass path (**23**) surround four beds (**24**) with the statue in the centre (**25**). The entrance (**26**), and the alcoves in the hedge (**27**) provide vistas to the statue, which gives height, so the obelisks are not needed.

8. COUNTRY HOUSE GARDEN

This is an outward-looking garden, set in the country; but it is on an irregular site which, to be formal, needs regularizing by the creation of a series of rooms and levels. The design is a combination of glamorous set pieces — each a horticultural triumph inviting admiration — and contrasting areas which are very straightforward. The garden's most distinctive feature is an avenue planted on a raised walk along one side of the house. The avenue is a neglected garden feature, often because it is mistakenly associated with grandeur of scale. But with the right sized trees or ones which can be pruned to shape, it is perfectly possible to have an avenue in quite a small space. Avenues add vertical accent as well as pattern to a garden. This particular one is only 80 feet (24 metres) in length and consists of eight pairs of trees annually clipped to form mopheads, but could as easily be formed by, for instance, pleached limes. The purpose here is to add an outdoor long gallery in which to stroll; it serves to frame two vistas which, if views are absent, could as easily be closed with a decorative artefact. An avenue is more often used to connect one part of a garden with another — an exciting option in planning. When planting an avenue it is worth growing one or two extra plants in a spare corner of the garden in case of losses in the early stages.

The avenue, visible from the first moment of planting, forms a marked contrast to the Topiary Yew Garden at the front of the house (see next page), which can never be anything other than a long-term project. This has been assigned to an area where it can gradually mature until it becomes one of the garden's most striking features — and a very inexpensive one at that, for all it requires is five young yew plants tucked into small beds in the turf. Patience does the rest, apart from annual feeding and clipping. A topiary yew garden bestows on any house a sense of style and distinction well worth waiting for.

The third set piece is an apple tunnel which closes the main vista from the back of the house. This offers an enclosed feature as opposed to the open experience of the avenue. From the moment that the framework is up the effect is visible and, like the avenue, its main demand is for careful annual pruning. It offers spring blossom and autumn fruit.

These set pieces are designed to lift what is otherwise a fairly ordinary garden with a large lawn, flowerbeds and a working kitchen garden. Should you wish for a potager you will need to rearrange the fruit trees and the beds to form a geometric pattern.

Apart from the initial landscaping and terracing this is not an expensive garden, bearing in mind its size. Nor is it particularly labour-intensive, for it offers a balance between areas of high and low maintenance. There are also wonderful opportunities for the naturalized planting of spring bulbs beneath the mature trees. The four herbaceous borders are crucial as they contribute the only floriferous aspect to the composition. The contrast between the drama and colour of those beds and the almost monochromatic Topiary Yew Garden, apple tunnel and avenue would be striking. The lawn area would make a successful garden in its own right but you would need to place something eye-catching where the steps lead to the apple tunnel. All the design features in this garden are easily adaptable to other schemes.

A STILT HEDGE

A stilt hedge of pleached trees is a splendid alternative to an avenue. It can define space with its distinctive shape, yet allows views to other parts of the garden as well as room for underplanting.

Pleaching is usually done with limes (*Tilia*) and stilt hedging with hornbeams (*Carpinus betulus*), both of which can be trained on horizontal tiers in simple planes (see pages 152–3). Hornbeams can be clipped with mathematical precision and the shape is maintained throughout the winter months as the leaves, which turn russet, are retained. Limes are deciduous, but they are fragrant in the summer and their foliage is handsome and their growth very rapid; there is also a different kind of satisfaction to be had in winter from their geometrically trained bare branches. Both limes and hornbeams could be trained to meet overhead to form a cloistered avenue or tunnel.

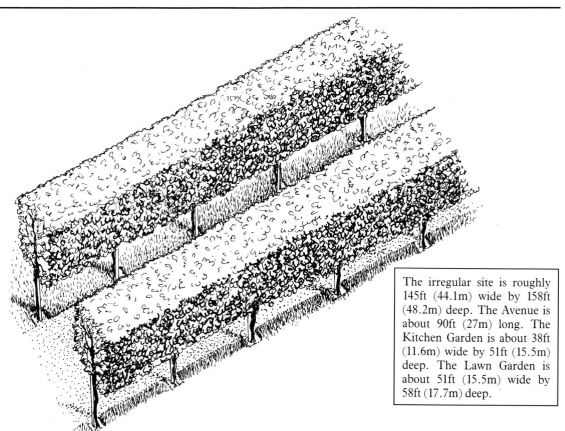

The irregular site is roughly 145ft (44.1m) wide by 158ft (48.2m) deep. The Avenue is about 90ft (27m) long. The Kitchen Garden is about 38ft (11.6m) wide by 51ft (15.5m) deep. The Lawn Garden is about 51ft (15.5m) wide by 58ft (17.7m) deep.

THE LAWN GARDEN

The lawn (**1**) is the same width as the house (**A**). It is surrounded by stone paths with some interest introduced at the corners (**2**) in the form of geometric patterns in brick and cobble. It has strong axes: one runs across the turf, through a gap in the beech hedge (**3**) which screens the kitchen garden, to an apple tunnel (**4**) with a seat (**5**) to close the vista; the other, running from north to south, has two seats facing each other, one (**6**) set into a bank and the other (**7**) consisting of an arbour of jasmine and honeysuckle, placed between two herb beds (**8**). Interest comes from the four symmetrically placed beds (**9**), containing a mixed planting which covers as much of the flowering season as possible; plan a framework of small shrubs such as hebes, senecios, phlomis, lavender, skimmias, *Cornus*, camellias, mahonias and the autumn-flowering *Ceratostigma willmottianum*, and fill in around them with a selection of perennials, biennials and annuals. Remember to control your palette, being cautious above all of the hot reds and bright oranges. The two herb beds (**8**) should not upset your colour scheme, for they are subtle in range. There it is important to establish a framework of plants which will form permanent architectural features, such as box and bay.

At the far end of the lawn, a path leads to a flight of steps (**10**) up to the avenue (**12**). From here it will be a delight to look down on the Lawn Garden. The opposite end of the path certainly calls for an eye-catcher of some kind (**11**) to close the vista.

THE AVENUE

This avenue is of the small-leafed evergreen *Quercus ilex* (**13**) trained as mopheads on trunks about 6 feet (2 metres) high, which will need pruning annually. Almost any tree can be pruned to form a mophead but a particularly attractive alternative would be *Robinia pseudoacacia* 'Inermis' which has the most beautiful fluttering palmate yellow-green leaves. Beech *(Fagus sylvatica)* is another possibility; as is *Amelanchier lamarckii*, which is deciduous but gives frothy white blossom in the spring and glorious colour in the autumn. A very different kind of avenue, less open at the base and very Italianate, could be made by planting narrow columnar conifers such as *Juniperus communis* 'Hibernica'. The path is of gravel but it could be paved. The view at one end is across a ha-ha (**14**) (a deep ditch with a wall down one side, a device which prevents animals crossing it but doesn't interrupt the view). A seat (**15**) is placed so one can look either along the avenue, or out over the surrounding landscape.

THE WILD GARDEN

A very good way to enhance the inherited bonus of mature trees (**16**) is to underplant them with drifts of spring and autumn bulbs. Planting bulbs is always hard work, so stagger it over a number of years, remembering to keep a rough plan in order to control position, colour, and flowering sequence. The grass will need to be left uncut until mid-summer if bulbs are to continue to flower and multiply from season to season. This sort of mowing regime will also allow other self-seeding plants such as primroses to multiply.

THE APPLE TUNNEL AND ORCHARD

Many fruit trees need to be planted close enough to compatible varieties to allow cross-pollination. Here there is a simple planting of trees (**17**) to one side of a major feature, an apple tunnel (**4**). The framework can be built of wood but it is easier and better to purchase one of those now available in plastic-covered metal. They can be made in a semi-circle or an ellipse at the top but the overall height should not be more than about 8 feet (2.4 metres), and the width of the path not more than 6 feet (1.8 metres). The trees should be trained as espaliers or cordons (see pages 154–5).

THE KITCHEN GARDEN

Hidden by a beech hedge (**3**) and in contrast to other parts of the garden this is quite simple; it is little more than a series of beds for vegetables (**18**), with room for a toolshed (**19**) and a compost heap beneath the large tree (**20**). If you would like a more decorative potager dispense with the apple tunnel and adapt the design given for the Potager in Garden 6 (page 116–7) or the designs for Garden 2 (page 106–7), closing the main vista with a little summerhouse.

THE TOPIARY YEW GARDEN

A topiary garden in yew (**21**) is a long-term investment that takes about fifteen years before the individual pieces assume the desired height and shape. Thereafter they will only call for annual clipping and feeding, thus forming a very low-maintenance garden. A topiary garden in yew is therefore an ideal solution for a secluded area of a larger garden where it can quietly reach maturity. Below are some typical traditional topiary shapes about 6-8 feet (1.8–2.4 metres) high, arranged to form a striking tableau that is balanced and broadly symmetrical. A myriad other shapes are possible: you could, for instance, strike out and create a garden of green Henry Moore sculptures!

Yew is best planted young. Larger plants take time to re-establish themselves and will soon be overtaken by ones planted much smaller. Do not expect much progress for the first five years but from then onwards growth will be rapid. Tying into shape may be called for (see pages 152–3). Prefabricated wire frames delineating the completed shape are available but not really necessary if you know the figure you are aiming for. It will take about ten years to get a really tangible effect. A topiary yew garden is evergreen sculpture on a grand scale and, when complete, will provide your garden with one of its greatest year-round spectacles.

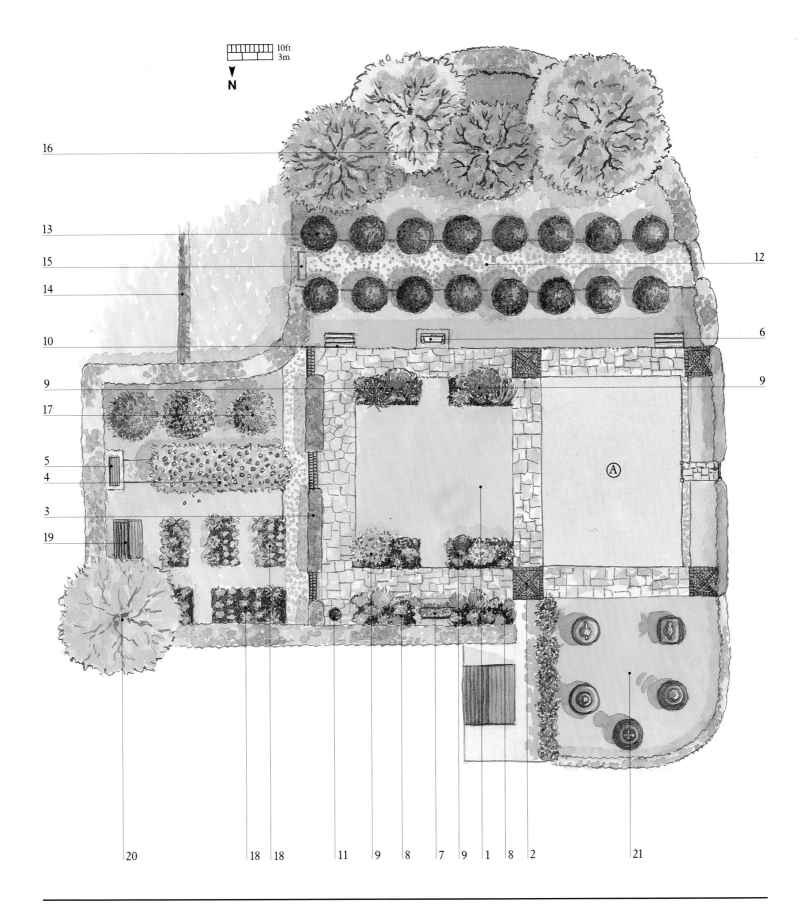

10ft
3m

N

16

13

15

12

14

6

10

9

9

17

A

5

4

3

19

20   18 18   11   9   8   7   9   1   8   2   21

9. COTTAGE POTAGER

Along narrow strip with a central path up to the front door is a characteristic shape for cottage gardens, and, surprisingly, it is perfectly possible to allocate within this tiny space not only a terrace for sitting out and for container plants but beds for flowers and for culinary herbs while the main body of the garden is given over to enough vegetables and fruit for at least two people.

Complicated patterns would be inappropriate for such a modest site and dwelling. The divisions should be of the simplest symmetrical geometric kind, accentuated with features which retain their presence for twelve months of the year: two fruit trees, topiary, standard roses and box balls or cones in pots. One of the most essential elements in a potager is the height provided by these features; otherwise the produce would only stretch out monotonously from the terrace to the front hedge. The aim of this scheme is to create a garden that would be attractive both as one walked up the path from the gate, and as one looked out from the house.

This plan could, of course, be used also for a long narrow back garden. If so the closing boundary hedge would need to be regularized and the path, working in reverse, would call for something to close the vista, such as a seat beneath a pergola, or one of the topiary pieces could be dropped and the other moved to the centre. The plan is also adaptable for an urban back garden, so many of which are made up of a similar long narrow strip. The potager section would be ideal for the furthest end, allowing for a pleasure garden next to the house.

Although small, this is a high-maintenance garden, but it is not expensive; the paving is simple and could be laid by the owner. It could be created almost instantaneously, except for the hedges and topiary pieces, but these should in any case be a joy to watch year after year as they gradually reach perfection. Anyone bent on a potager will need to be a committed gardener and, in order to succeed in making the effect decorative, must be fully conversant with the rotation of crops necessary for produce. Although this garden is firm on structure (with four alternative designs to choose from) it is essentially a seasonal garden — a fact that will have been taken into consideration at the outset. Such a garden is still unusual, and will continue to come as a great surprise and delight to the visitor.

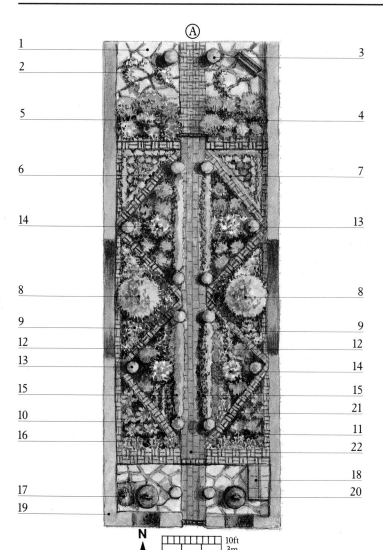

THE POTAGER

The terrace (**1**) just outside the front door of the house (**A**) looks down the whole length of the potager. As it faces south, it is ideal for sitting out on and for container plants such as tender indoor geraniums to pass the summer, and for other container plants such as lilies and fuchsias. Ground-hugging thymes could be planted in the gaps between paving stones (**2**). Box balls in containers (**3**) flank the front door and sweet-smelling climbers are assumed to smother the cottage walls. A herb bed (**4**) is sited where it would benefit most from the warmth of the sun, with a bed opposite (**5**) in which to plant a bouquet of old-fashioned cottage garden flowers, delphiniums, paeonies, hellebores, geums, pinks and hollyhocks, with a few spring bulbs.

In proximity to the front door there are two beds for salad stuff: one edged with parsley (**6**), the other with chives (**7**). Seasonal plantings for the salad bowl included here are lettuce, chicory, radicchio and spring onions. Half-way down the garden, height is given by two fruit trees (**8**): both are apples, one a cooker, the other an eater. They should be on dwarf rooting stock (MM 26) which will give an overall spread of about 10 feet (3 metres). Two compatible trees are needed to ensure pollination. In the beds (**9**) beneath them I would place a naturalistic spring planting of crocus, daffodils and narcissi which could be followed in the summer by *Geranium psilostemon*, *Campanula persicifolia* and *Aquilegia vulgaris*. Other beds can be given over to rhubarb (**10**) with globe artichokes and blackcurrants (**11**) as more permanent features, while the remaining beds (**12**) will be subject to crop rotation and could include courgettes (zucchini), French beans, mangetout (sugar peas) and 'Pink Fir Apple' potatoes. Before you embark on your planting, decide what you wish to grow, make a plan and establish your rotation system.

The design is given accent and height by box balls in containers (**13**) which are sited at the corners of the beds, and by standard roses (**14**) planted at four of the centres. I would suggest perhaps *Rosa* 'Pascali' which is a beautifully formed white Hybrid Tea rose or *R.* 'Iceberg', a white floribunda which flowers freely over a long season. A definite edging to the

N
▲   10ft
     3m

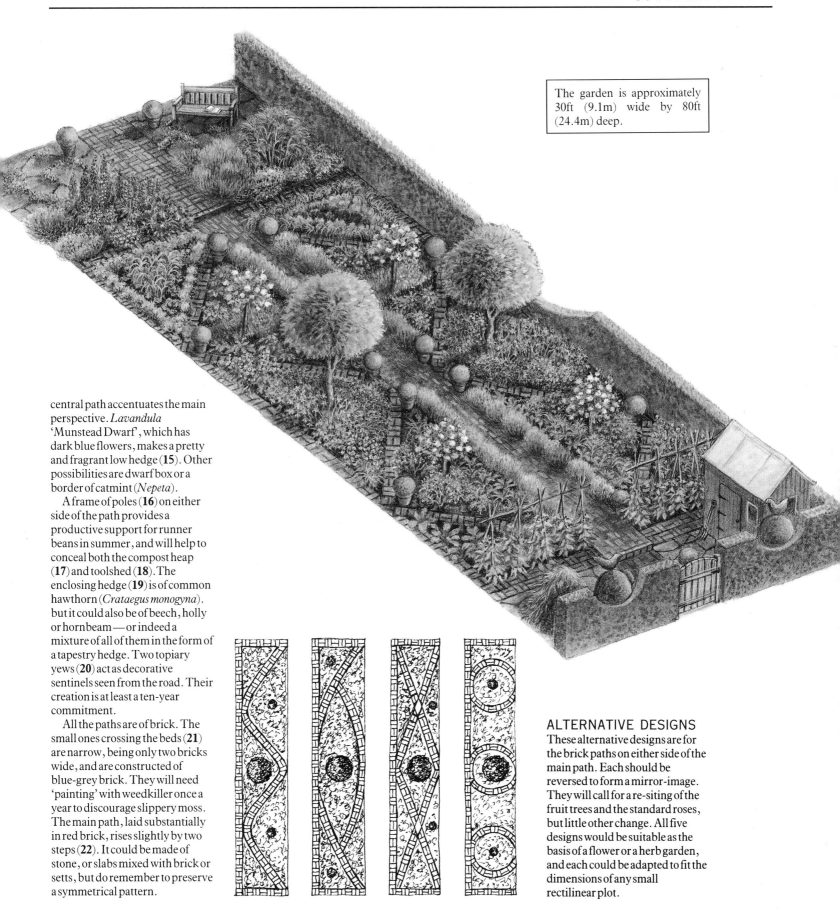

The garden is approximately 30ft (9.1m) wide by 80ft (24.4m) deep.

central path accentuates the main perspective. *Lavandula* 'Munstead Dwarf', which has dark blue flowers, makes a pretty and fragrant low hedge (**15**). Other possibilities are dwarf box or a border of catmint (*Nepeta*).

A frame of poles (**16**) on either side of the path provides a productive support for runner beans in summer, and will help to conceal both the compost heap (**17**) and toolshed (**18**). The enclosing hedge (**19**) is of common hawthorn (*Crataegus monogyna*). but it could also be of beech, holly or hornbeam — or indeed a mixture of all of them in the form of a tapestry hedge. Two topiary yews (**20**) act as decorative sentinels seen from the road. Their creation is at least a ten-year commitment.

All the paths are of brick. The small ones crossing the beds (**21**) are narrow, being only two bricks wide, and are constructed of blue-grey brick. They will need 'painting' with weedkiller once a year to discourage slippery moss. The main path, laid substantially in red brick, rises slightly by two steps (**22**). It could be made of stone, or slabs mixed with brick or setts, but do remember to preserve a symmetrical pattern.

ALTERNATIVE DESIGNS

These alternative designs are for the brick paths on either side of the main path. Each should be reversed to form a mirror-image. They will call for a re-siting of the fruit trees and the standard roses, but little other change. All five designs would be suitable as the basis of a flower or a herb garden, and each could be adapted to fit the dimensions of any small rectilinear plot.

10. TINY COTTAGE GARDEN

This particular garden was designed for a tiny croft in Scotland. The house was built on a very exposed site where the land falls away steeply, so that in order to create any garden at all the earth had to be banked to form a square terrace the width of the croft's front. This raises a garden design problem which occurs also in the cold and often quite barren climate of Scandinavia and parts of North America, where the winters are very severe and the ground can be under snow for several months. Often these stone-built houses or log cabins are second homes used for winter sports and summer holidays. Their attraction lies in the surrounding landscape, like the steep hills covered with pine trees, heather and bracken with outcrops of rock upon which this croft looks out.

Gardening in these circumstances can never be more than a summer occupation and the achievement of a succession of bloom within these months would be a triumph. Such an achievement would be emphasized by a formal treatment of the garden space to link house and garden into a symmetrical frame for the display of precious plants. A formal architectural scheme, by the well-proportioned design of its built elements, gives pleasure during all those months when there is little plant life. Indeed, this is the strongest argument for formalizing such a site.

For such a modest house the detailing should aim at an unpretentious charm. The materials used for the paving, important at all times of the year, must relate to those of the house and, ideally, should be local. As the beds will be without plants for much of the year they should be laid out in a strong geometric pattern and given interest by a decorative edging. Frost-proof brick laid on a diagonal is one solution; rope-tile edging would be another. Give the garden a definite but not too grand centrepiece. Choose a simple circular urn or planter, avoiding any of classical style which would be out of keeping with the rusticity of the croft.

Such a composition calls for a definite boundary to draw attention to its character as an oasis of cultivation in the wild. This can be done by planting a striking hedge. Here, it is evergreen berberis with a pair of fastigiate Irish yews as sentinels at the two far corners; an alternative would be a tapestry hedge of two varieties of beech.

The colourful element in the garden, being almost totally a summer phenomenon, is made up of hardy plants that will stand up to cold and exposed conditions. A permanent framework of shrubs and perennials could be embroidered with a planting of hardy annuals during the warm summer months.

There are several other geometric layouts among the designs in this book which would be equally suitable for such an area, including the potager within Garden 7 (page 118) and both parterres for Garden 2 (pages 106–7). Much will depend on the space available and amount of time you can give to it which, because the garden can only ever be seasonal, may only be five months of the year. Apart from the initial landscaping this is an inexpensive garden and requires relatively low maintenance.

THE GARDEN

The garden is enclosed by an evergreen hedge (**1**) of *Berberis × stenophylla* which is extremely hardy and will quickly give you a dense hedge of green leaves with golden-yellow flowers in the spring. The two Irish yews (**2**) (*Taxus baccata* 'Fastigiata') will slowly ascend and form stately sentinels, giving a perfect balance to the garden from a distance and framing the house and gate. They are slow-growing initially but then quickly rise to about 8 feet (2.4 metres) in ten years if regularly fed. If you prefer there is a golden variety, *T. b.* 'Aurea', which is glorious in winter sun.

A rose, *Rosa* 'Albertine' (**3**), has been planted to grow up the wall of the house (**A**) which will give a display of bloom in mid-summer. You may prefer to choose hardy wall shrubs such as *Chaenomeles*, *Garrya elliptica*, *Pyracantha* or *Jasminum nudiflorum*. Other climbers to consider are species and varieties of clematis and *Hydrangea petiolaris*.

Within, the garden is paved to form a series of beds edged with frost-resistant brick laid edge-to-edge in a diagonal (**4**). The four spandrel beds (**5**) could each take the same hardy shrub, and the centre bed (**6**) another. Choose those which will not grow too large or which can be regularly pruned. Here a potentilla, which has a long flowering period, occupies the central bed, while the rest contain *Fuchsia magellanica*, one of the hardiest fuchsias which, even if cut to the base in winter, will spring up and flower the next season. It may help to protect the crown with straw during the coldest winters.

With shrubs as a framework, you could add, for instance, some early bulbs — snowdrops and crocus — and bedding plants or hardy perennials for a summer display. I suggest a Veronica planted with the potentilla, violets and pansies to fill space in the spandrel beds, while the central urn (**7**) contains petunias and lobelia.

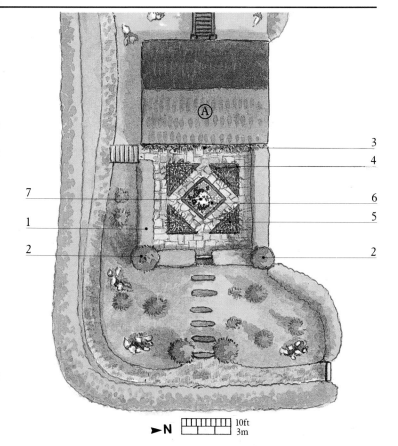

►N 10ft / 3m

The garden is about 20ft (6m) square within the enclosing hedge.

11. MONDRIAN PARTERRE

Formality need not be expressed in terms of historicism. Contrary to belief it can speak in the idiom of the twentieth century in an equally vigorous and exhilarating way. With imagination a whole new parterre tradition can be invented by mining the quarry of contemporary art. This was the inspiration of the small town back garden shown here. It was designed for a modern house with a garage, a kitchen on the ground floor and the main living room above. The windows of the living room look down on the pattern of the garden's centrepiece, a raised parterre inspired by Mondrian's paintings. Piet Mondrian (1872–1944) was a Dutch painter who evolved an extremely rigorous style of Abstraction known as Neo-Plasticism, which consisted in restricting forms to purely geometrical shapes and setting them at right angles to the horizontal or vertical axes. Colour was restricted to the three primary ones, red, yellow and blue with white, black and grey. It is, of course, impossible to reproduce the colour scheme of a Mondrian painting in horticultural terms, but the division of his pictures into rectilinear areas infilled with colour is marvellously adaptable for a box parterre with block planting.

This is the inward-looking town garden of a family house, so beyond the set piece there is an ample lawn flanking a central path as the main axis to a symmetrically disposed pattern of hard and soft surfaces and planting. An area for open-air living closes the vista with a summerhouse and a small sculpture court. It is a great disappointment that there are no mass multiples of contemporary sculpture suitable for the garden as there are of reconstituted stone ornaments in the classical style. The little sculpture court is designed to encourage the owners to become patrons and to buy a bronze piece and really enjoy its response to light and the play of the seasons. The summerhouse, framed by two flowering *Prunus*, needs to be strictly modern in feeling, slightly austere — as should the rest of the garden.

Ideally this garden, in which hard surfaces and built features are so important, calls for professional landscaping. That would be a major expense but you would have a virtually instant garden, while the planting would reach maturity within five to eight years. Further maintenance is minimal, only requiring seasonal mowing and pruning. The parterre is the only major commitment for it would require planting once a year with a painter's eye for the disposition of the blocks of colour. But then anyone embarking on such a project would be reckoning on the challenge in the choice of plants as half the enjoyment.

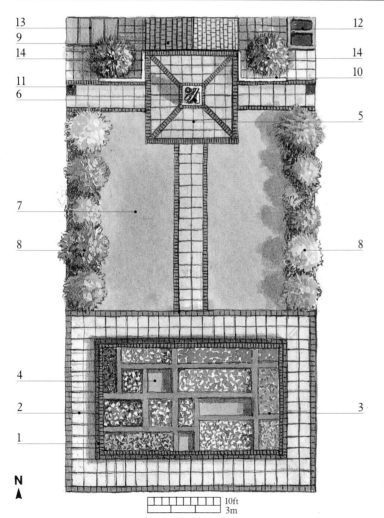

THE MONDRIAN PARTERRE

Nothing should distract from the formal beauty of the composition which is therefore conceived as a raised bed of brick (**1**) surrounded by paving (**2**). There are no distracting climbers on the flanking walls, which could, if it appeals, be painted white. If you are not lucky enough to have walls, clothe trellis with dense green ivy. The compartments (**3**) of the parterre are formed of carefully clipped dwarf box (*Buxus sempervirens* 'Suffruticosa'). Three of them (**4**) should be filled with gravel, not only to form a contrast but also to facilitate access for weeding and planting. The remainder call for a spring and summer planting in the strong colours typical of Mondrian's pictures. Here it is of yellow, red and white tulips. In summer it could be of annuals with a long flowering period, such as petunias, pelargoniums or impatiens. Whatever you choose, remember to fill a preponderance of the compartments with flowers of one colour, preferably white, or the result will be too hectic.

THE SCULPTURE GARDEN

The elements of this are very simple. Paving (**5**) is laid in a pattern of slabs and bricks to lead the eye to the sculpture (**6**), and areas of mown grass (**7**) have a shrubbery (**8**) on either side. It is important to avoid shrubs with colours which might compete with the parterre; rather they should be chiefly evergreens with white, very pale pink or cream flowers, and could include *Viburnum tinus*, some of the escallonias, *Elaeagnus × ebbingei*, *Choisya*, *Philadelphus*, *Cotoneaster × watereri*, *Cistus × cyprius*, *Hydrangea quercifolia*, *Euonymus japonicus* 'Duc d'Anjou', *Elaeagnus angustifolia*, *Hebe pinguifolia* 'Pagei', *Hibiscus syriacus*, *Daphne retusa*, *Hebe salicifolia*, *Euonymus fortunei* 'Silver Queen', *Daphne × burkwoodii*. The summerhouse (**9**) and flanking trellis screens (**10**) should be painted white. If you want to soften the austerity of the garden you could train ivy up the trellis, or a honeysuckle which would give fragrance. The summerhouse is so distant from the parterre that other options are

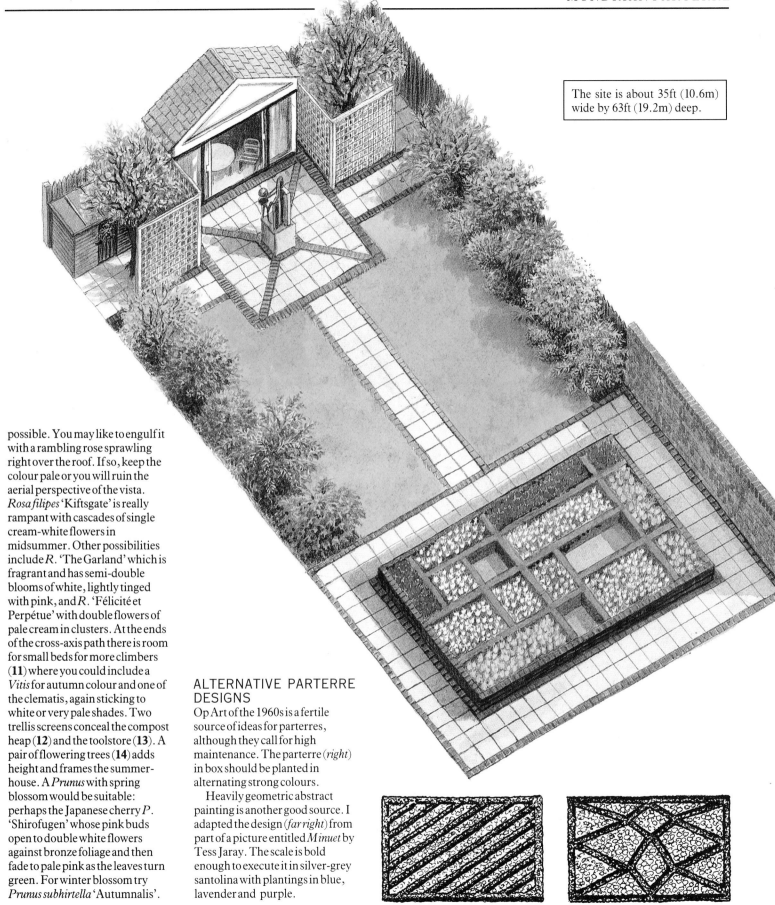

possible. You may like to engulf it with a rambling rose sprawling right over the roof. If so, keep the colour pale or you will ruin the aerial perspective of the vista. *Rosa filipes* 'Kiftsgate' is really rampant with cascades of single cream-white flowers in midsummer. Other possibilities include *R*. 'The Garland' which is fragrant and has semi-double blooms of white, lightly tinged with pink, and *R*. 'Félicité et Perpétue' with double flowers of pale cream in clusters. At the ends of the cross-axis path there is room for small beds for more climbers (**11**) where you could include a *Vitis* for autumn colour and one of the clematis, again sticking to white or very pale shades. Two trellis screens conceal the compost heap (**12**) and the toolstore (**13**). A pair of flowering trees (**14**) adds height and frames the summer-house. A *Prunus* with spring blossom would be suitable: perhaps the Japanese cherry *P*. 'Shirofugen' whose pink buds open to double white flowers against bronze foliage and then fade to pale pink as the leaves turn green. For winter blossom try *Prunus subhirtella* 'Autumnalis'.

ALTERNATIVE PARTERRE DESIGNS

Op Art of the 1960s is a fertile source of ideas for parterres, although they call for high maintenance. The parterre (*right*) in box should be planted in alternating strong colours.

Heavily geometric abstract painting is another good source. I adapted the design (*far right*) from part of a picture entitled *Minuet* by Tess Jaray. The scale is bold enough to execute it in silver-grey santolina with plantings in blue, lavender and purple.

12. ART DECO PARTERRE

Art Deco was the last style in this century to produce a repertory of decoration in everything from textiles to metalwork, from wallpaper to ceramics. As a style it was current from about 1918 to 1939, expressing a composite response to a new more liberated society, to new living styles and to new technology. The style was a synthesis of exotic influences: lingerings of turn-of-the-century Art Nouveau, Bauhaus, African ethnic art, Cubism, the art of ancient Egypt and the Aztecs and the impact of the Russian ballet. It made only a limited impression on garden design but it seems to me to offer the most wonderful array of patterns for parterres.

The fountain motif was one of the most all-pervasive Art Deco motifs symbolizing the life process ascending from some mysterious source and returning to it. This parterre is based on a textile design of 1927 by Edward Benedictus (1878–1930) in which gold jets of water are set against a brick-red background.

This is a front garden with a vista from the gate to the facade of the house. If you use it for a back garden you would need to close the vista from the house at the gate end. If you have less space, you could drop the central fountain and half the parterre but keep the two symmetrical areas of grass and the tree as they offer crucial contrast to the parterre. Such an ambitious and glorious garden would inevitably be expensive, but the result from the first would be stunning. It would be complete within about five to eight years and needs amazingly little maintenance. The effect depends upon the pattern made up of green box and purple berberis with ivy as groundcover in the compartments. This is a decorator's garden: an unashamed celebration of the subjection of nature to art.

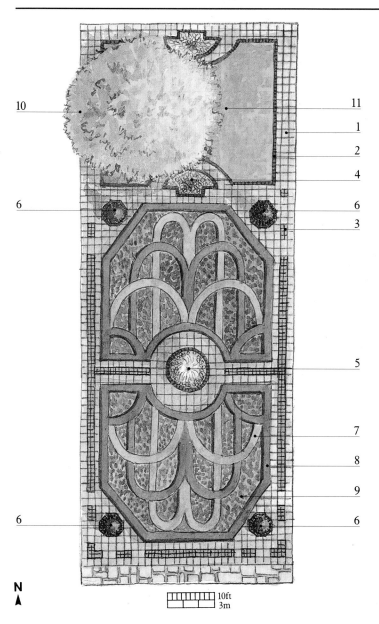

N
▲

|||||||||| 10ft
3m

THE ART DECO PARTERRE

The hard surfaces of this garden use variegated paving laid in patterns of the period: stone or simulated stone (**1**) with brick (**2**), setts (**3**) and cobbles (**4**) to accentuate the geometry. The parterre is given height by the central fountain (**5**) and four fastigiate evergreens (**6**) at the corners. I would suggest using *Juniperus virginiana* 'Skyrocket' which is possibly the narrowest of all the columnar conifers and has handsome blue-grey foliage. Other possibilities are *Chamaecyparis lawsoniana* 'Columnaris Glauca' which also forms a narrow column but in blue and green shades; or *Taxus baccata* 'Fastigiata', the upright Irish yew. The parterre is laid out in dwarf box (*Buxus sempervirens* 'Suffruticosa') (**7**) and the reddish-purple *Berberis thunbergii* 'Atropurpurea Nana' (**8**). The trimming time of both vary. Box should be cut in early summer, berberis in late summer. You could consider using an evergreen dwarf berberis instead of the box or, as the berberis is deciduous, you might perhaps prefer to plant the parterre in two sorts of box, the ordinary green *Buxus sempervirens* and either the golden (*B.s.* 'Gold Tip') or the silver-grey with leaves edged in silver (*B.s.* 'Elegantissima'). More ephemeral possibilities such as lavender cotton (*Santolina chamaecyparissus*) are ruled out because they need replacing every five or so years, which would be too labour-intensive.

This parterre calls for groundcover in the compartments (**9**) and the ivies would seem a natural choice. The Persian ivy *Hedera colchica* has the largest leaf of any and it would be a striking contrast to the tiny leaves of the box and berberis. On the whole I would not personally favour a flowering groundcover but if that is your choice *Vinca minor* 'Bowles Variety' with its pretty light blue flowers between late summer and mid-autumn might look quite striking.

If you want blocks of brighter colour, the two alternative designs (*right*) would lend themselves more willingly to block planting in spring and summer. The large tree (**10**) is a demonstration of how existing features can be incorporated into a formal scene. In its likely absence you will be able to plant a pair of trees centred on each area of grass (**11**). As there are so few flowers in the rest of the garden the choice of a flowering tree would be attractive. I would favour a pair of magnolias such as *Magnolia stellata*, which is slow-growing but flowers when young. One of the white flowering cherries, such as *Prunus* 'Shirotae,' or *P.* 'Shirofugen' (which has bronze young foliage), would be equally appropriate and correct for period.

The garden is about 45ft (13.7m) wide by 115ft (35.0m) deep.

ALTERNATIVE DESIGNS

The design (*above left*) for a semi-circular Art Deco parterre in box is based on a 1925 plate by Jean Luce. It employs an archetypal Art Deco motif of sunrays and clouds, and would be well suited to block planting within the compartments. The square design (*left*) for an Art Deco parterre in box incorporates a step motif familiar from Aztec art. This would also lend itself to block planting.

13. URBAN THEATRE

The narrow rectangular strip at the back of a house is a common feature all over the world, particularly where there is terrace housing dating from the last century. Inevitably such a garden will be inward-looking. There is not that much privacy to be had when there is an almost identical site abutting on all three sides, so that the temptation to use the garden as an open-air room will be limited.

The main part of this garden is so small that a lawn would not only look ridiculous but would also present totally unnecessary maintenance problems. A garden of these minute dimensions cannot be used to wander in, but it can be designed to be something to wonder at, if you make it into a tableau which gives the illusion of increased space and add a planting which will give something of interest for all twelve months of the year.

This garden depends on false perspective to achieve that illusion. Firstly, the vista is accentuated at ground level by the pattern of the paving in which lines of brick have been made to converge gently — a convergence which is emphasized in the summer months by the placing and colour of plant containers. But the main manipulation of the space is by the use of wings or buttresses of evergreen or of treillage to lead the eye to the back of this stage set, which therefore must have a dramatic focal point. Here it takes the form of a portable *trompe l'oeil* figure of a lute-playing lady but it could equally be something sculptural: a bust on a plinth, a column with a finial or an urn on top. Whatever you choose should be set off to advantage in a treillage arch. Use the same colour to paint the remaining trelliswork on the walls, which is designed to support climbers that will soften the severity of the architecture.

If you choose treillage wings, this garden is virtually instant. If you opt for the evergreen wings you will have to wait for them to mature, but then you will have the enjoyment of training them into shape. The paving and treillage would represent a heavy initial financial outlay and unless you are very accomplished it would be better to have it carried out by a craftsman or builder. The maintenance, however, is minimal; the main tasks would be annual pruning and looking after the plant containers.

► N 10ft / 3m

THE GARDEN

Close to the house (**A**) is a bed which would be good for culinary herbs (**1**). There would also be room for an espaliered apple tree (**2**), if there was another in the vicinity to ensure cross-pollination. Beyond that a terrace of quarry tiles (**3**) stretches the full width of the garden.

The main garden is paved in different coloured slabs and bricks (**4**) laid in a pattern that takes one's eye to the end of the garden. The area is incised by two pairs of evergreen wings (**5**) of Portugal laurel (*Prunus lusitanica*), which must be pruned with secateurs to avoid savaging the leaves with shears. It has dense rich dark green leaves and, if you are lucky, tassels of scented white flowers in mid-summer followed by dark purple berries. Other possibilities include *Thuja plicata* 'Atrovirens', which grows very fast but is somewhat unexciting, or yew (*Taxus baccata*) which is slower but would be very beautiful.

The other planting consists chiefly of flowering climbers to soften the architecture and provide colour. A possible scheme would be: for the north-facing wall a *Clematis montana* (**6**), or a *Jasminum nudiflorum* if you want winter colour, and a *Hydrangea petiolaris* (**7**), which has frothy white flowerheads in summer; opposite, on the south-facing wall honeysuckle (**8**), perhaps two plants, *Lonicera periclymenum* 'Belgica' and *L.p.* 'Serotina,' the early- and late-flowering Dutch honeysuckles with marvellously scented flowers, and a repeat-flowering rose, such as the pale apricot-pink *Rosa* 'Gloire de Dijon' (**9**). All the climbers could be underplanted (**10**) with bulbs, and annuals or easily maintained perennials. The trellis arch at the end could also support climbers such as clematis. The flowers should be small to compound the illusion of distance; I would choose the early flowering blue *Clematis alpina* 'Frances Rivis' (**11**), and the later-flowering yellow *Clematis tangutica* (**12**). A pair of small flowering trees (**13**) at the far end will give height to the garden. I would suggest *Sorbus aria* or *Malus* 'Golden Hornet'. The focus of the garden is, however, the *trompe l'oeil* figure (**14**), which is painted *en grisaille* on wood. Two pairs of flower-filled containers would soften the architectural effect of the paving and if planted with hotter colours in the foreground (**15**) and cooler blue or mauve flowers further back (**16**), would help to increase the illusion of depth.

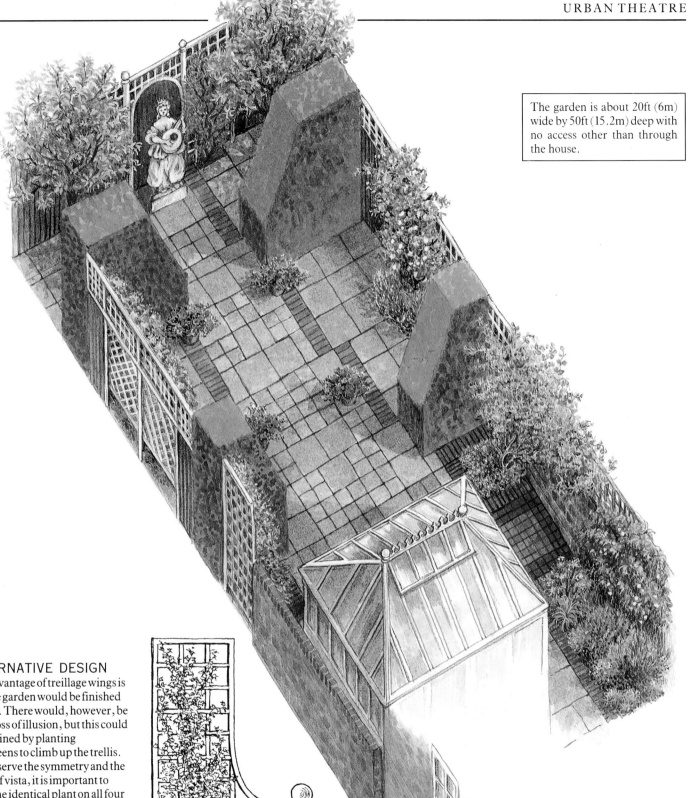

The garden is about 20ft (6m) wide by 50ft (15.2m) deep with no access other than through the house.

ALTERNATIVE DESIGN

The advantage of treillage wings is that the garden would be finished at once. There would, however, be some loss of illusion, but this could be regained by planting evergreens to climb up the trellis. To preserve the symmetry and the effect of vista, it is important to grow the identical plant on all four wings. As the wings are meant to act as a foil to the flowers, green leaves are all that is required and one of the ivies would be ideal. My preference would be for one with dark green leaves; the variegated varieties would be restless against the trellis.

14. KIOSK GARDEN

A cursory glance may relegate this garden design to the realms of Arabian Nights fantasy rather than practical reality. In fact it illustrates a general principle which can be applied in a wide range of circumstances, where an illusion of formality needs to be superimposed on an irregular area of woodland or random planting. The solution is to make a focal point — in this instance an exotic kiosk — and create a vista to it. The vista may be framed by clipped hedges or an avenue; or, as here, by both — a hedge of yew with an avenue of lemon trees in large terracotta pots. To emphasize the formality a pair of cypresses has been planted within the concealed natural habitat.

This orchestration of the site to draw it into a formal composition is applicable anywhere in the world. It is only the planting and the built features that may be different. In colder countries the same effect could be achieved in a plantation of fir or pine trees by clearing a pathway to a small classical temple or pretty summer-house, or even a simple feature such as an obelisk or column, and planting a hedge of hornbeam or yew.

In this particular case, the climate is warm and the area quite small. The garden has two parts, both inward-looking. A courtyard has been formalized into a symmetrical outdoor cloister with a pergola for climbers on all four sides. In the middle there is a cooling fountain with a single jet, very much in the Islamic tradition, surrounded by containers for seasonal planting. A decorative ironwork screen divides the two parts, and a gate leads to a path in stone and brick that echoes the central courtyard. An equivalent effect could be achieved with treillage, to complement a simple wooden kiosk, and a path in gravel and brick.

This is not a high-maintenance garden. The hedge will need annual clipping but the natural planting it conceals requires relatively little work. The cost of initial capital works, including paving and built features, will be high, even if more modest main features are substituted. The effect, however, would be almost instant, only the hedge needing time to mature. There would be few times of the year when this garden would not be attractive and the more exciting the building the more pleasing it would be.

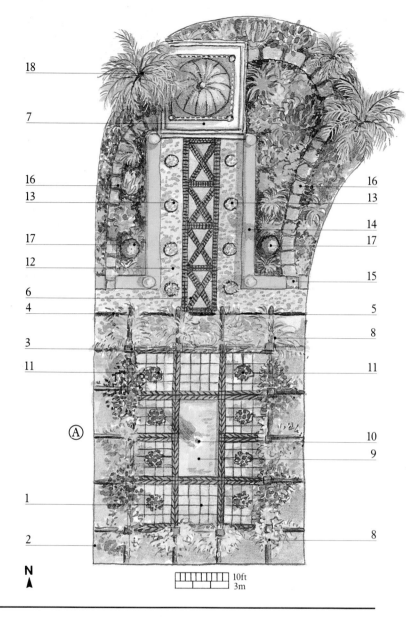

THE COURTYARD

The courtyard (**1**) is bounded by the house (**A**) and walls (**2**) on three sides but is open to the north where the pergola columns (**3**) are linked by means of a series of decorative ironwork screens (**4**) to a pretty pair of gates (**5**) which open on to the path (**6**) to the kiosk (**7**). There would be room to dine in the shade of the cloister formed by the pergola.

The pergola supports are of brick with wooden rafters, and there are beds at the base for climbers (**8**). Wisteria would be my first choice of climber sited to provide a curtain of gorgeous lilac, blue, purple, pink or white flowers in spring through which to view the vista. In a warm climate, vines and bourgainvillea might be suitable, or many other tender climbers, including such exotic jasmines as the long-flowering yellow *Jasminum mesneyi* or the white and deliciously scented *Jasminum polyanthum*. Another possibility would be *Campsis radicans*, the scarlet trumpet vine.

In the centre there is a rectangle of water (**9**), with a single jet (**10**). In eight of the paved squares there are pots (**11**) for seasonal planting.

THE KIOSK GARDEN

Opening off the centre of the pergola is a walk of stone and brick (**6**) flanked by an area of gravel (**12**), formalized with an avenue of lemon trees (**13**). In some areas these will have to be taken in during the winter months. Many other plants could be substituted including standard fuchsias or blue or white agapanthus. The yew hedge (**14**) is only about 3 feet 6 inches (1 metre) high, making it possible to peer over and see the luxuriant wild area. There are entrances (**15**) to this part of the garden on both sides and winding paths (**16**) to the kiosk. Two Italian cypresses (*Cupressus sempervirens* var. *stricta*) (**17**) frame the kiosk from a distance, and the area is planted with an array of sun-loving trees, shrubs and groundcover plants. The palm (**18**) provides the height needed to set off the kiosk.

The kiosk (**7**) is made of fretwork in the Moorish Islamic style. A simple alternative design in the Gothick style (**19**) is also given. Whatever is built should have a touch of fantasy and stand in its own right as an object. To cover it with climbers would only repeat the effect on the pergola.

The walled Courtyard, including the pergola, is roughly 40ft (12.2m) wide by 45ft (13.7m) deep. The Kiosk Garden is an irregularly shaped area about 50ft (15.2m) wide by 55ft (16m) deep.

19

15. WILDERNESS AND MAZE GARDEN

T his garden at first glance might seem a wild extravagance, but it opens up exciting possibilities for those who suddenly find themselves with a large site and would like to find a way of making a substantial part of it dramatic and unusual but also supremely manageable. An original solution would be to plant a modern version of a seventeenth-century wilderness.

Today that word conjures up an image of the wild gardens of William Robinson and Gertrude Jekyll, where an area beyond the immediate vicinity of the house was planted in such a way that it seemed to merge gradually into the surrounding landscape. The seventeenth-century wilderness did exactly the reverse: it deliberately emphasized the contrast between the landscape outside and cultivated nature within. It occupied an area of land that was divided by means of hedges and groves of trees into rooms and passages. The rooms might contain flowering trees, a seat or indeed an ornament as a focal point. The treatment was geometrical, combining a series of secret enclosures with spectacular perspective vistas that made it the most wonderful place in which to walk. The cunning disposition of the hedges and trees gave the impression that it was far larger than was the reality.

In this garden, which is sited in a sunny climate, the purpose is a specific one: to give those who use the pool a wonderful pattern to look down upon and cool shady walks in which to stroll. The staircase down is Italianate in the grand manner and for its construction the help of an architect and a builder would be needed. But its splendours speak for themselves.

The wilderness and maze are placed in precise symmetry flanking a vista towards the staircase. Endless variants of both are possible but of the two it is the wilderness which has the greatest potential, for its hedges could be cut into interesting shapes and small trees could be planted in formal patterns in the 'cabinets'. A maze is a delicious eccentricity. It is not essential to look down on it, although not only the idea but also the pattern itself is appealing, and it can be fun to see where people have got to.

The maze here is of yew. It would take fifteen years from planting to become impenetrable but you would be able to pace out its intricacies from the start, provided that you did not cheat by stepping over a hedge. The wilderness, which is in beech, would give a pleasant colour contrast in winter with its russet leaves. Apart from the mowing, the biggest commitment would be the huge annual task of clipping for which labour could be hired in.

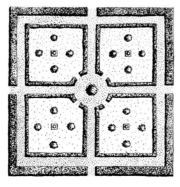

ALTERNATIVE DESIGNS

These designs are for areas about 80 feet (24 metres) square.

The maze design comes from the famous architectural treatise of Sebastiano Serlio (1475–1554). Allow for hedges of about 6 feet (1.8 metres) high and 3 feet (90 centimetres) wide, and paths of 3½ feet (1 metre) wide.

The wilderness is enclosed by a yew hedge with gravel walks around and quartering it. Plant a handsome specimen tree or build a celebratory column as a central focal point. Four rooms enclosed by beech hedging open off the central circus, and each should have something like an obelisk as a focal point surrounded by small flowering trees. The yew hedge could be clipped into an ornamental shape (see page 138), but beech is better left straight.

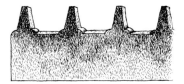
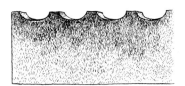

ORNAMENTAL SHAPES FOR HEDGING

Few features of a formal garden give greater satisfaction than hedging. We are so obsessed with instant effect in this century that we have forgotten the joy of watching hedges grow to maturity, training and shaping them. Our ancestors lived far shorter lives. In the golden age of formal gardening, most would have been dead by forty but no one hesitated to devote ten to fifteen years of that span to making a garden.

The designs for hedges are almost limitless and, although you should always make a plan of how you ultimately intend to shape it, be prepared to modify or even alter your ideas as the hedge matures. The eye is the surest guide of all. Do not regard hedge clipping as a chore. You should set out to enjoy every minute over the years as you shape what will be one of your most stunning garden features. If you have inherited an old hedge which is boring, you may be able to reshape it. Approach with caution but yew, especially, is remarkably tolerant.

All the designs are best executed in yew (*Taxus baccata*), which, if fed regularly, can reach a height of about 6 feet (1.8 metres) in ten years. If you are quite determined to have much faster results western red cedar (*Thuja plicata*) or leyland cypress (× *Cupressocyparis leylandii*) would be viable alternatives. If you are aiming for a hedge of less majestic proportions, to make a division within a garden, for instance, the first three designs could be shaped in box (*Buxus sempervirens*); the scallops would be particularly attractive on a smaller scale.

THE PERGOLA AND POOL

The pergola (**1**) is of classical columns in reconstituted stone with wooden beams between them. The ideal plant to clothe it would be wisteria, with its cascades of pale lilac or white flowers, feathery foliage and wonderful trunk formation. For a different colour scheme trumpet vine (*Campsis radicans*), with its clusters of scarlet and orange trumpets, would be a handsome alternative. For autumn colour a vine could be added: *Vitis coignetiae*, a very vigorous species, is unrivalled for the brilliant orange and crimson shades of its leaves; *V. vinifera* 'Brant' turns crimson-orange and then pink, while *V. v.* 'Purpurea' turns a claret and later a rich vinous-purple. The pergola offers a shady place to sit, and might also be used to conceal a pool house.

Pools (**2**) need an uncluttered surround. Here containers (**3**) add summer colour with seasonal plantings and pots could be placed on the piers of the balustrading (**4**). They will, however, require regular watering. If you wish to emphasize the formal symmetry you might place box cones in the containers at the corners.

THE STAIRCASE AND CROSS-AXIS

The drop is of 10 feet (3 metres) allowing for a spectacular staircase (**5**). The terracing must be done professionally but the component parts of the scheme can be purchased from manufacturers of reconstituted stone architectural parts. In the central arch (**6**) a little grotto with a fountain could be made and, as the two flanking walls (**7**) face south, they would be ideal for espaliered fruit trees or

climbers. I would favour *Magnolia grandiflora* 'Exmouth', a plant of the right scale with large evergreen shiny leaves and richly scented cream-coloured goblet-shaped flowers all summer. There is also room to introduce another pair of trees, should you so wish; as this particular garden is in a warm and sunny region, palms would be lovely. I would favour, however, just leaving this area as a beautiful gravel walk.

THE MAZE

The maze is of yew (*Taxus baccata*). Allow the hedges (**8**) to grow about 3 feet (90 centimetres) in width and 6 feet (1.8 metres) in height so that you cannot see over them; and it is traditional to keep them straight at the top. It would seem prudent to have gravel walks within (**9**) as mowing could be a tiresome task. The gravel would only require a periodic raking and the application of weedkiller. In the middle there is a statue (**10**) but a small flowering tree is another possibility.

THE WILDERNESS

The wilderness is divided from the maze by a gravel path. Here the hedges are of beech (*Fagus sylvatica*) (**11**). Hornbeam (*Carpinus betulus*) would be another possibility. Both keep their leaves in winter, and the beech preserves them till springtime. Grass paths are essential as a contrast, and I would suggest close-cutting the axis paths (**12**) and the outer oval (**13**), and rough-cutting the central oval (**14**) and the two 'cabinets' (**15**). In the centre there is a complementary statue (**16**) but, again, you could have a small flowering tree. Similar trees could

be introduced in the outer oval, two in each of the 'cabinets' and one in each of the four closed triangles (**17**), to which you must contrive a small entrance for maintenance. Whatever you chose should rise above the hedges and be a trophy of pretty blossom in the spring and perhaps of autumn fruits too. Possibilities include, according to your climate and soil conditions, the full range of flowering cherries (*Prunus*) and crab apples (*Malus*). Two seats (**18**) at either end of the main axis of the wilderness are placed to enjoy the vista.

The overall size of the garden is about 100ft (30.4m) wide by 150ft (45.6m) deep. The Pergola and Pool terrace is 100ft (30.4m) wide by 50ft (15.2m) deep; the Staircase and the Cross-axis gravel path together measure 100ft (30.4m) wide by 20ft (6m) deep. The Wilderness and Maze are each about 40ft (12m) wide by 75ft (22m) deep with a gravel path dividing them. There is a drop of 10ft (3m).

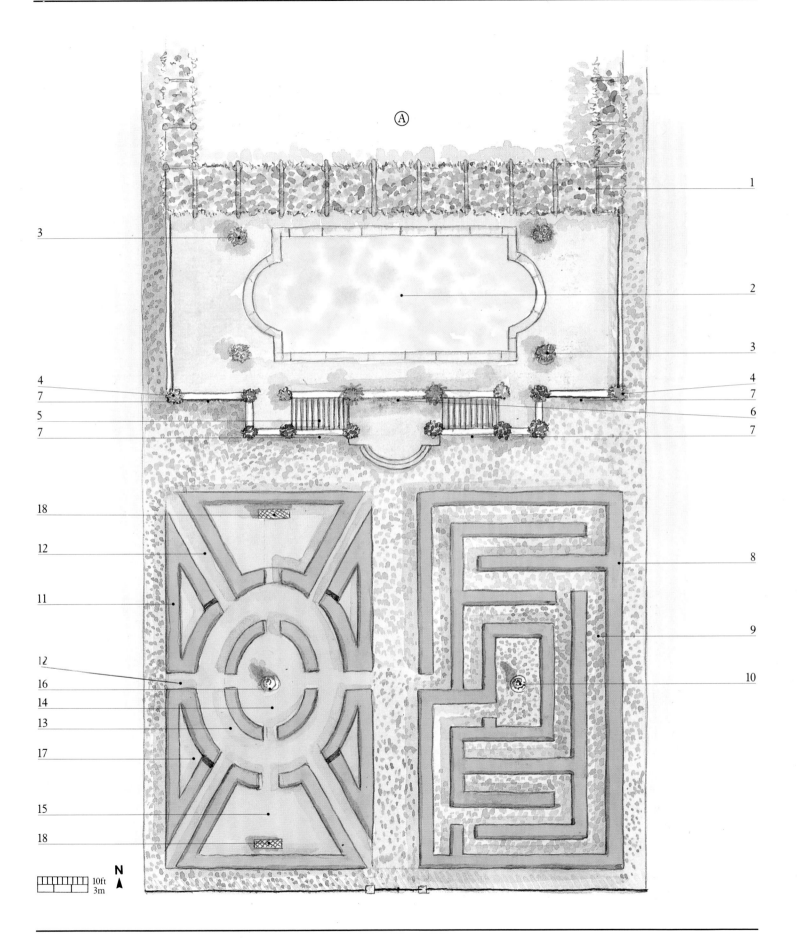

Ⓐ

1

3

2

3

4
7
5
7

4
7
6
7

18

12

11

8

9

12
16
14
13
17

10

15

18

N

10ft
3m

16. COURTYARD GARDEN

This tiny courtyard is only 18 feet (5 metres) square and yet it has been possible to fit into it a planting varied enough to cover the seasons, together with a small fountain. This type of courtyard is familiar in the urban environment of hot countries. Inevitably it is inward-looking, here it is no more than a paved area between the gate leading out to the street and the front door but often it will be at the back or side of the house. And yet it is a precious space in which to sit, and, during the day in summer, shelter from the hot sun is essential.

To establish formality start at ground level with the paving. In such a small area its quality matters. Its geometry will form the basis for the composition of the whole space. The focal point, a small fountain, takes up the pattern vertically and containers placed in symmetrical pairs emphasize it further.

In two of the corners there are beds for climbers. As this design is for a hot climate, they are trained over the network of wires to form a ceiling of this 'room'. In cooler climates climbers would be trained up trellis attached to the walls. Although small, this is a garden which calls for commitment, as every detail is in close focus and containers cannot be neglected for as much as a single day. An alternative to the central fountain would be one in a wall, as in Garden 18 (page 145) which could be surrounded by plants arranged as a set piece. If possible, site it where it will always be seen from a window of the house. If a wall fountain is not a possibility try to achieve some kind of decorative arrangement on one wall: trellis arches, perhaps, focussing on a figure or a plaque in relief.

N ◄

3ft
1m

THE COURTYARD

At ground level the courtyard is articulated by geometrically patterned paving (**1**) which emphasizes, by two square lines of brick (**2**), the shape enclosing the central cobbled area (**3**). This contains a small fountain with a single jet (**4**) and an octagonal pool. This needs to be fairly low as nothing should be placed in the centre to interrupt the view across the whole space. The fountain brings with it the attractive and refreshing movement of water. With a simple electrically operated pump its maintenance would be minimal. There are, however, alternatives. One is to leave the centre empty and replace the fountain with a really interesting paving pattern or, if you are feeling extravagant, commission a mosaic. Another would be to have a really splendid planter. Once again it should not be more than about 3 feet (1 metre) high. A large terracotta one decorated with masks and swags would be ideal,

but keep the planting low and add compensating interest in the way of trailing plants such as the ivies or pelargoniums.

Overhead wires are stretched to support two climbers, a *Wisteria sinensis* (**5**), which has wonderful trunk and branch formations and fragrant pale lilac-purple flowers succeeded by yellow-green leaves, the other a vine (*Vitis*) (**6**) which will give leafy shade in the summer months and glorious tints in the autumn. These are a personal choice but, depending on the aspect of your walls, you can select two climbing plants from among the very large range. Choose them to contrast with each other and give foliage and flowers at different times of the year.

Space for containers is limited. As with the climbers, container gardening offers a whole world of choice in which you can freely follow your personal preference. Here I have placed a single tub of the evergreen *Fatsia japonica* (**7**) and three pairs of containers with

aspidistra (**8**) on either side of the seat, mock topiary (**9**) on either side of the gate (**B**), and pelargoniums (**10**) on either side of the front door of the house (**A**). The mock topiary adds a permanent formal feature and is easily achieved by training ivy over a wire frame in the form of a corkscrew.

Container gardening is highly labour-intensive, for it requires regular watering, changes of soil and sometimes two seasonal plantings in a single container. It can also quickly become very untidy, so I would counsel having only a few good, reasonably large containers, well placed and well maintained, rather than a confused plethora. To highlight formality some of these pairs at least should be of strongly formal plants such as standard fuchsias, clipped box or bay.

A courtyard such as this may need lighting after dark. The fountain could look very pretty if lit from within the water.

ALTERNATIVE DESIGN

If the fountain and pool were not wanted, it is important that the design for the paving is strong, as well as geometric, as it will become the most important permanent feature of the garden. The pattern here comprises square and triangular slabs of stone, brick, and cobbles.

The courtyard is 18ft (5.5m) square. In the eastern wall there is a gate out to the street; on the north side is a blank wall and the walls of the house form the remaining two sides with a front door in the centre of the western wall.

17. BALCONY PARTERRE

The very idea of an apartment balcony, penthouse terrace or roof garden might at first seem totally at variance with the idea of formal gardening, and yet the basic principles of symmetry, vista and pattern can all be applied enormously successfully to a tiny aerial space. Indeed, not only can they be used to make a stunning outdoor room with perennial appeal, but also to create the illusion of greater space than is really the case.

In no other format is a garden so cheek by jowl with the living rooms — in fact they often make a continuum and flow into each other by means of French windows or sliding glass doors. This means that the design of a balcony garden will in some way be dictated by the decoration of the interior; it can also, by extension, enhance it. A pair of classical urns symmetrically placed on a terrace can, for example, carry the theme of a room decorated in the country-house style optically beyond the windows. The shape and type of containers and the colours of the plants you use, and, even more, the design and colour of your outdoor furniture should be influenced by your interior schemes. It is no use having a drawing room in a symphony of ochres, pale yellows and white and placing outside the window containers with shocking pink flowers and bright blue deckchairs. The result will be a horrendous colour clash. Similarly a modern interior calls for streamlined outdoor furniture rather than lacy wrought-iron work.

The proximity of your living room means you will be looking out over your balcony all through the year, making it even more important that the garden provides unfailing interest. That, indeed, is one of the most fundamental requirements of any successful formal garden scheme. So, start with the basic geometry and permanent structures, and base your planting on a backbone of clipped evergreens such as bay or box, or naturally disciplined plants like skimmia, or even some of the slow-growing dwarf conifers of columnar shape. Your initial approach will depend upon whether your balcony has a marvellous view or whether it has one which in part at least you wish to obliterate. For instance, containers with formal clipped evergreens can be arranged outside a window as an 'avenue' to draw the eye and frame a particular view. Or an abundant use of treillage with climbers, perhaps to create a sense of theatre (see page 132), can make the area inward-looking, distracting the eye from less pleasant surroundings. The most important thing is to base your plan on the view of the balcony from your windows and doors.

So much of formal gardening depends on geometric groundplanning that it might seem impossible to achieve in a balcony garden. In fact that problem can be overcome by tiling the floor area in an interesting pattern. An exciting option would be to make a 'parterre' in which one colour represents the 'hedges' and the other the 'earth'. You will need to draw a careful groundplan on graph paper, taking into account the views from the room and remembering that your containers must sit comfortably within the tiled layout. I give two designs here, but it would be easy to find other plans throughout this book which could be adapted.

Great attention should be paid to the containers, as they will assume a far greater prominence than when they are set among other plants in a larger garden. Spend as much as you can afford on

them, since they will be permanently on display. But before you buy any, check the load-bearing potential of your balcony. Many suppliers now make 'lead' and 'painted wood' classical urns and tubs in fibreglass which is light and easy to move.

The many opportunities presented by the walls should be exploited. Treillage, painted a colour subtly contrasting with the wall, can either stand in its own right or it can support climbers. If the floor is strong enough, roses and honeysuckle and a great number of other climbing plants will flourish in containers. Simply to clothe a wall, however, my preference would be for a variegated ivy, which is tolerant of neglect, breaks up the surface and provides year-round interest. A wall will also enable you to include garden sculpture in the form of a mask or plaque, or even a small wall fountain (see page 144).

There are, however, many constraints on balcony gardening: exposure to the wind, the need for light containers, for drought-resistant plants, for somewhere to hide your few tools and a disposal system for weeds, dead plants and exhausted earth. This negative side should be recognized from the outset, for a really gorgeous balcony garden calls for constant love and attention — a single dead bloom assumes an importance which would be hardly noticeable in an ordinary garden.

Yet the small size of most balconies means that with the right structural ingredients, including a preponderance of evergreen plants, it need not require a disproportionate amount of maintenance. Instead, it can offer a surprising number of exciting opportunities for the urban gardener.

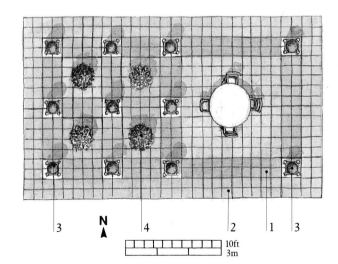

3   N   4   2   1   3

10ft
3m

THE PARTERRE GARDEN
The garden is divided into two parts: one is an area for sitting, and the other has been made into a formal parterre by the pattern of the floor tiles. Green tiles stand for the 'hedges' (**1**) and brown for the 'earth' (**2**) and paths. Eleven Versailles tubs containing box

clipped into domes or balls are placed at the corners and crossings (**3**). The four 'flowerbeds' (**4**) have containers for seasonal plantings. They can be instant in the fullest sense, filled in succession with purchased pot plants from the local nursery or market: pansies in the winter, hyacinths in spring,

The balcony is 30ft (9.1m) long and 18ft (5.5m) wide.

pelargoniums in summer and fuchsias perhaps in the autumn — whatever is available as long as the colour is right. If you are unsure about colour, however, stick to white, using plants with a long flowering period. If your colour scheme allows, it would be lovely to add some scented plants to enjoy while sitting outside.

ALTERNATIVE DESIGN

The basic principle of establishing your 'parterre' in the paving of your balcony can be adapted to any number of patterns and symmetrical arrangements of plant containers, but you must always preserve a strong evergreen framework, and to work from the vista of the inside room outwards.

18. BASEMENT GARDEN

A basement garden has much in common with one on a balcony. In both cases they are primarily something to look out upon from within the house or apartment. With a basement area, it is certainly the view that counts, for no one would sit out there and there is no view beyond. Basement gardening is real picture-making, generally in adverse horticultural circumstances. The achievement of some glorious illusion is therefore all the more of a triumph by its maker for he will have had to come to grips with a narrow and shady space which by its very nature greatly restricts the choice of plants to those that can thrive without much sun and be content in containers.

The basement for which this design was made is typical of many nineteenth-century town houses which have a flight of steps leading down to what was once the tradesmen's entrance. Nowadays the steps generally lead to the front door of a basement-level flat. It is always the outlook from any windows giving on to the basement that must determine how the space is treated.

First and foremost it is essential to get as much light as possible by painting the walls a light colour, white or pale cream. Next the space must be given a decorative structure which will be charming to look out on even if there are no plants. Trellis, which is inexpensive, is ideal for this, but you may need the services of a carpenter to cut it to shape. Green is a good colour suggesting foliage but green-blue can be just as attractive. A simple wall fountain opposite the window (a statue or bas-relief plaque would do equally well) holds the design together, providing a focus to the view.

The planting, here accommodated in four symmetrically placed Versailles tubs, serves to complement the permanent features. Remember that the life of plants will be finite and that the earth will have to be disposed of and replaced from time to time. A multiplication of planters is only a multiplication of problems. The aim of a basement garden is to evoke the idea of a garden rather than to carry it out in reality; and, in the main, it has to do this through elements other than plants.

The treatment could be enlarged for a small town garden which has only a confined paved area, although in that case attention should be paid to making the paving of some interest. This could be achieved by extending the treillage and multiplying the tubs, rather as in the Baroque Parterre (see pages 40–3).

THE BASEMENT GARDEN

The main point of the garden is the tableau as seen through the window of the house (**A**) directly opposite the wall fountain and lion's mask (**1**). The walls should be painted white, off-white or pale cream, to make the most of the light that filters down. The grey-green trellis (**2**) should be mounted sufficiently clear of the wall to allow plants to be tied into the trellis, and to make it easier to remove to repaint the walls.

The most important single feature of this scheme is the focal point of the view. A wall fountain is not a major expense although plumbing the water pipes into the wall calls for professional help. The system works by means of an electric motor which recycles the water and can be operated by a switch from within the house. As you will almost certainly have some form of electric light for the basement steps, you might consider adding a sense of theatrical drama to the tableau at night by putting in spotlights to fall on the plants when they are in bloom, and particularly on the water. There is almost nothing to compete with the visual appeal of moving water, even on this scale, but if plumbing work is out of the question for you, an alternative focal point would be a small plaque above a decorative trough planter (*illustrated above, right*).

The four Versailles tubs (**3–6**), which are available in fibreglass and look like wood, are here painted a sophisticated glossy black. Finding plants that will thrive in these circumstances is not easy. I would favour flanking the tableau with a pair of evergreen shrubs. My first choice would be camellias (**3** and **4**) which have beautiful glossy leaves and flower all spring. They are hardy, thrive in moist shade, and will reach a height of about 6 feet (1.8 metres) when pot grown. There is a very wide range of varieties to choose from, with pink, red or white, single or double flowers. An alternative would be *Fatsia japonica* which has boldly shaped shiny leaves and white flowers in the autumn, and also reaches 6 feet (1.8 metres) in height.

Against the house wall there are two further tubs, one for perhaps the evergreen *Clematis armandii* (**5**) and the other for a jasmine (**6**). Both the winter-flowering *Jasminum nudiflorum* and the summer-flowering *Jasminum officinale* can be successfully container grown. Both are deciduous, but one will reward you with small yellow flowers all through the winter, and the other with exquisitely scented white flowers in the summer.

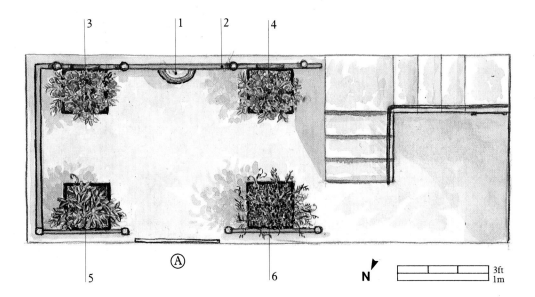

3   1   2   4

Ⓐ

5   6

N   3ft / 1m

ALTERNATIVE FOCAL POINT

Fill the trough with flowering plants that do not compete either in colour or season with those in flanking tubs. Another alternative would be a bust on a plinth, but town life being what it is these days it would be advisable to stick to something which is not likely to be stolen or vandalized.

The area, excluding the steps down, is only 9½ft (2.9m) long and 6ft (1.8m) wide with a wall 9ft (2.7m) high.

THE PRACTICALITIES OF FORMALITY

Formal gardening not only demands the skills usual to ordinary gardening but also those which raise garden making into an art: fluency in sculpting hedges with shears, laying out and caring for a parterre, espaliering fruit trees, pleaching, or trimming trees to mopheads and training topiary to shape. As you gain in confidence and master each of these techniques you will feel yourself assume a kind of horticultural superiority, for you will have begun to learn the language of a great tradition, much of which has lain dormant or much diminished in this century. In the old days such skills were passed down orally from one generation to another. That broken descent now has to be replaced by the dedicated work of the garden owners themselves.

In the absence of a living craft tradition, horticultural experts cannot agree in their recommendations for methods of achieving particular effects. When I began to create a formal garden fifteen years ago, I literally had to guess what these techniques might be. None of my yew hedge, for example, was ever trained with the recommended sloping batter to its sides. But the hedge is there all the same and the thinner areas at the bottom have filled in. Do not be afraid to experiment with your own methods and do not despair at making a mistake.

In making a formal garden there is one labour and skill you must learn to love above every other, and that is clipping and pruning. Once a year there will be a cutting of hedges and topiary (in summer) and a pruning of trees (in winter). But it is a thrilling task to see longed-for shapes emerging or being restored.

PLANTS FOR FORMAL GARDENS

I do not go into planting in any detail in this book. Not only does this depend on climate, soil, aspect and access to supply, but on personal choice — and half of the fun of gardening is choosing plants and following their progress. But there are recurring elements in the designs in this book which pertain particularly to formal gardening, and the following lists suggest a selection of plants under those categories.

Symbols and zones

○   prefers full sun
○◐   will do well in sun or partial shade
○   prefers light shade
○◐   tolerates full shade
z = zone

Plants have been allocated zones, which are ranges of temperature in which they are likely to survive, fruiting and flowering satisfactorily, although aspect, site and amount of moisture will also have an effect.

Zone	Fahrenheit	Centigrade
1	below −50°	below −46°
2	−50° to 40°	−46° to −40°
3	−40° to 30°	−40° to −34°
4	−30° to 20°	−34° to −28°
5	−20° to 10°	−28° to −22°
6	−10° to 0°	−22° to −16°
7	0° to 10°	−16° to −12°
8	10° to 20°	−12° to −6°
9	20° to 30°	−6° to −1°
10	30° to 40°	−1° to 4°

Shrubs for screening and privacy

(Mixed borders could, of course, include perennials and ground cover plants: the choice is so wide that any basic selection would be meaninglessly limited.)

Evergreen shrubs

Zone	Symbol	Plant
z 6–10	○◐	Abelia × grandiflora
z 5–9	○◐	Berberis species eg B. darwinii
z 7–9	◐●	Camellia species and cultivars especially C. × williamsii hybrids
z 7–9	○	Ceanothus species and cultivars eg C. thyrsiflorus 'Repens'
z 6–9	○◐	Choisya ternata
z 8–9	○	Cordyline australis
z 5–10	○◐	Cotoneaster dammeri
z 6–10	○	C. × watereri
z 6–9	○◐	Cryptomeria japonica 'Elegans'
z 8–10	○	Daphne odora
z 6–9	○◐	Elaeagnus pungens
z 7–9	○◐	E. ebbingei
z 6–9	○◐	E. macrophylla
z 8–9	○	Escallonia × iveyi 'Apple Blossom'
z 7–9	○◐	Eucryphia × nymansensis
z 8–10	◐●	Fatsia japonica
z 7–9	◐●	Garrya elliptica 'James Roof'
z 8–10	○	Hebe species and cultivars eg H. 'Midsummer Beauty'
z 6–9	○◐	Ilex aquifolium
z 6–9	◐●	Mahonia japonica
z 8–10	○	Myrtus communis
z 7–9	○	Osmanthus delavayi
z 7–9	◐	Pieris 'Forest Flame'
z 8–10	○	Pittosporum tenuifolium
z 7–10	○●	Prunus lusitanica
z 5–9	◐	Rhododendron species and cultivars eg R. yakashimanum
z 7–9	◐	Sarcocca hookeriana
z 7–9	◐●	Skimmia japonica
z 6–9	○●	Stranvaesia davidiana
z 6–9	○●	Viburnum tinus
z 5–9	○◐	V. × burkwoodii

Deciduous shrubs and small trees to provide flowers and/or autumn colour

Zone	Symbol	Plant
z 5–9	○	Amelanchier lamarkii
		Azaleas see Rhododendron
z 6–9	○	Ceratostigma willmottianum
z 5–9	○◐	Chaenomeles japonica
z 7–9	○◐	Cornus alba 'Elegantissima'
z 5–9	○	C. kousa chinensis
z 5–9	○	Cotinus coggygria
		Cytisus praecox
z 7–9	○	C. × kewensis
z 6–9	◐	Daphne mezereum
z 5–9	○	Deutzia × hybrida
z 7–9	○	Fuchsia magellanica
z 5–9	◐	Hamamelis mollis
z 6–9	○	Hibiscus syriacus
z 5–9	◐	Hydrangea quercifolia
z 7–9	○◐	Kolkwitzia amabilis
z 6–9	○	Malus eg × 'John Downie'
z 7–10	○◐	Paeonia lutea ludlowii
z 6–9	◐	Potentilla fruticosa
		Prunus species especially
z 6–9	◐	P. sargentii and
z 6–9	◐	P. serrulata spontanea and other flowering cherries
z 6–9	◐	Ribes sanguineum
		Rhododendron eg Knap Hill and Exbury hybrids
		Sorbus species especially
z 4–8	○◐	S. aucuparia and
z 2–8	◐	S. hupehensis
z 6–9	○◐	Spiraea × arguta
z 7–10	○◐	Viburnum plicatum 'Mariesii'
z 5–9	○◐	V. × bodnantense
z 6–10	○◐	Weigela florida and hybrids

'Evergrey' or 'everblue' shrubs

Zone	Symbol	Plant
z 7–9	○	Artemisia 'Powis Castle'
z 8–10	○	Ballota pseudodictamnus
z 7–10	○	Convolvulus cneorum
z 7–9	○	Olearia macrodonta
z 7–9	○	Phlomis fruticosa
z 7–10	○	Rosmarinus officinalis
z 8–10	○	Ruta graveolens 'Jackman' Blue'
z 7–9	○	Salvia officinalis
z 8–10	○	Yucca filamentosa

Evergreen climbers and wall plants

Zone	Symbol	Plant
z 7–9	○	Artemisia arborescens
z 7–9	○	Ceanothus species

and hybrids eg *C.* × 'Autumnal Blue'

z 7–9	○	*Clematis armandii*
z 8–10	○●	*Euonymus fortunei* 'Silver Queen'
z 7–10	○●	*Hedera helix*
z 6–10	◐	*Lonicera japonica*
z 6–8	◐●	*Pileostegia viburnoides*
z 6–8	○◐	*Pyracantha coccinea* 'Lalandei'
z 8–10	○	*Tecomaria capensis*
z 8–10	○	*Trachelospermum jasminoides*
z 8–10	○	*T. asiatica*

Deciduous climbers and wall shrubs for flowers and foliage

z 8–10	○◐	*Abutilon* × *suntense*
z 7–9	○	*Actinidia kolomikta*
z 7–9	○	*Akebia quinata*
z 7–9	○◐	*Ampelopsis aconitifolia*
z 10	○	*Bougainvillea* species and hybrids
z 5–10	○	*Campsis radicans*
z 7–9	○○	*Ceanothus* 'Gloire de Versailles'
z 6–9	○◐	*Chaenomeles speciosa*
		Clematis species eg
z 3–9	○◐	*C. alpina*
z 4–7	○◐	*C. macropetala*
z 4–7	○◐	*C. montana*
z 6–9	○	*C.* large-flowered hybrids
z 8–9	○	*Cytisus battandieri*
z 4–9	○◐	*Forsythia suspensa*
z 7–9	○	*Humulus lupulus* 'Aureus'
z 4–9	◐	*Hydrangea petiolaris*
z 8–10	○	*Jasminum officinale*
z 6–10	◐●	*J. nudiflorum*
z 9–10	○	*J. polyanthum*
z 6–10	◐	*Lonicera* species and hybrids eg *L. periclymenum* 'Belgica' and 'Serotina'
z 7–9	◐●	*Parthenocissus henryana*
z 3–9	○◐	*P. quinquefolia*
z 9–10	○	*Passiflora caerulea*
z 7–9	○	*Rosa* climbers (generally repeat-flowering)
z 7–9	○	*Rosa* ramblers (generally flowering once only in a season)

z 8–9	○	*Solanum crispum* 'Autumnale'
z 6–9	○◐	*Vitis vinifera* 'Brant' and 'Purpurea'
z 6–10	○	*Wisteria floribunda*
z 6–9	○	*W. sinensis*

Formal hedging plants
(see page 39 and pages 148-9)

Trees suitable for pleaching and making stilt hedges
The tree to be used above every other is the lime, *Tilia.*

z 6–9	○	*Tilia cordata*
z 6–9	○	*T. platyphyllos* 'Rubra'
z 6–9	○	*Platanus orientalis*
z 8–9	◐	*Quercus ilex*

Trees suitable to train as mopheads and 'umbrellas'
Of the many trees that can be pruned to shape the following are particularly suitable:

z 5–8	◐	*Cornus mas*
z 5–9	○	*Crataegus* species and cultivars
z 5–9	◐	*Euonymus fortunei* 'Emerald Gaiety'
z 7–9	○●	*Ilex aquifolium* cultivars
z 9–10	◐	*Laurus nobilis*
z 7–10	○◐	*Prunus lusitanica*
z 6–9	◐	*Quercus ilex*
z 6–9	○	*Robinia pseudoacacia* 'Inermis'

Fruit trees and bushes suitable for training
The training that is needed to make fruit trees yield satisfactory crops is often highly ornamental, and the controlled shapes, free-standing or wall-trained, fit in well with the discipline of formal gardening. Varieties on dwarfing rootstocks are particularly suitable for small gardens where there is good cultivated soil.

z 7–9	○	Apples are the most versatile fruit tree for training, being suitable for growing as fans, cordons, espaliers, step-over hedges and various free-standing shapes.
z 7–9	○	Pears are almost as versatile as apples but their vigour makes them less suitable for the more restricted forms of training.
z 8–10	○	Peaches and apricots are particularly suited to fan training on walls, which helps the ripening of fruit in cooler areas.
z 7–9	○	Sweet cherries and plums can be fan trained but need plenty of room.
z 7–9	○	Acid cherries are suitable for fan training even in small gardens.
z 8–10	○	Figs need warmth for their fruit to ripen; they do best on a sunny wall.
z 8–10	○	Gooseberries are among the best of the bush fruits for training as cordons or standards.

Plants for containers
Plants grown in containers provide the formal gardener with material that allows great flexibility in the arrangement of patterns and tableaux. Short-term colourful planting can include bulbs, annuals, biennials and tender perennials. For long-term planting there are, in addition to evergreens suitable for shaping, such as a box, Portugal laurel and sweet bay, many shrubs with interesting foliage or flowers. The following lists include evergreens (E) and deciduous plants (D).

Compact and slow-growing conifers

z 3–8	○	*Abies balsamea* 'Hudsonea' (E)
z 5–8	◐	*Chamaecyparis lawsoniana* 'Ellwoodii' (E)
z 3–8	○	*Chamaecyparis pisifera* 'Boulevard' (E)
z 4–8	○	*Juniperus chinensis* 'Variegata' (E)
z 4–8	○	*Juniperus communis* 'Compressa' (E)
z 2–8	○	*Pinus mugo* 'Gnome' (E)
z 6–8	○	*Taxus baccata* 'Standishii' (E)
z 2–8	○	*Thuya occidentalis* 'Rheingold' (E)
z 6–8	○	*Thuja orientalis* 'Elegantissima' (E)

Flowering plants

z 8–10	○◐	*Agapanthus* 'Headbourne Hybrids' (E)
z 7–9	○◐	*Camellia* species and cultivars (E)
z 8–10	○	*Daphne odora* 'Aureomarginata' (E)
z 7–9	○◐	*Hydrangea macrophylla* mophead (hortensia) cultivars (D)
z 7–10	○◐	*Mahonia japonica* (E)
z 8–10	○	*Myrtus communis* (E)
z 8–10	○	*Nerium oleander* (E)
z 7–9	◐	*Pieris formosa* 'Forrestii' (E)
z 5–9	○◐	*Rhododendron* small species and cultivars (D and E)
z 6–9	○	*Rosa* miniature cultivars (D)

Plants with interesting foliage

z 7–9	○◐	*Acer palmatum* 'Dissectum' (D)
z 8–10	○	*Agave americana* (D)
z 8–10	○	*Cordyline australis* (E)
z 8–10	○●	× *Fatshedera lizei* (E)
z 8–10	○◐	*Fatsia japonica* (E)
z 7–9	○	*Hebe cupressoides* (E)
z 5–9	○●	*Hedera helix* cultivars (E)
z 5–10	◐●	*Hosta sieboldiana* 'Elegans' (E)
z 8–10	○	*Melianthus major* (D)
z 9–10	○	*Phormium cookianum* (E)
z 8–10	○	*Yucca filamentosa* (E)

Fruit

z 7–9	○	apples on M27 rootstocks (D)
z 8–10	○	figs (D)
z 7–8	○	gooseberries (D)
z 9–10	○	lemons (E)
z 9–10	○	oranges (E)

ORNAMENTAL HEDGING PLANTS

BERBERIS × STENOPHYLLA

Evergreen, very hardy and tolerant, it has glossy leaves, and arching sprays of golden-yellow flowers in spring if it is not pruned after mid-summer. It quickly makes a dense, dark green hedge if regularly trimmed.
GROWTH RATE: reaches 3–4ft (90–120cm) in 3 years and 6–8ft (1.8–2.4m) in 6 years.
PLANTING: set 18in (45cm) apart, in mid/late autumn or early spring, in sun or light shade.
SHAPING: trim by one half immediately after planting and trim top and side shoots each year in early summer to promote good bushy growth.

BERBERIS THUNBERGII 'ATROPURPUREA'

Deciduous hardy shrub with superb rich bronzy red summer foliage which turns brilliant scarlet in autumn. Dwarf forms include *B.t.* 'Atropurpurea Nana'.
PLANTING: Set 18in (45cm) apart (*B.t.* 'Atropurpurea Nana' 9–12in (20–25cm) apart), mid-autumn to early spring, in sun or light shade.
GROWTH RATE: reaches 3–4ft (90–120cm) (*B.t.* 'Atropurpurea Nana' 15in (45cm)) in 3 years and 5.6ft (1.5–1.8m) in 5–6 years.
SHAPING: trim by one half immediately after planting and trim top and side shoots each year in early summer.

BUXUS SEMPERVIRENS
(common box)

Evergreen and compact shrub with luxuriant small bright green leaves which responds well to clipping. *B.s.* 'Suffruticosa', is the dwarf form.
GROWTH RATE: reaches 3ft (90cm) in 3 years and 5–6ft (1.5–1.8m) in 6 years. (*B.t.* 'Suffruticosa' reaches 12in (30cm) in 3–4 years.)
PLANTING: set 15in (45cm) apart (*B.s* 'Suffruticosa' 4–6in (10–15cm) apart), in mid-autumn or early spring, in sun or light shade.
SHAPING: trim in early summer.

× CUPRESSOCYPARIS LEYLANDII

Evergreen, hardy, tolerant and fast-growing conifer with grey-green foliage, which soon makes a tall, dense hedge.
GROWTH RATE: reaches 3–6ft (90–180cm) in 3 years and 8–12ft (2.4–3.6m) in 6 years.
PLANTING: set 30in (80cm) apart, in autumn or spring, in sun or light shade. Stake the young plants.
SHAPING: use secateurs (hand pruners) to trim side shoots, especially when the plants are young, and do not pinch out the main shoot until the intended height is reached. Trim during the summer as necessary.

FAGUS SYLVATICA
(common or European beech)

Deciduous, hardy plant with leaves which are bright green in spring, darker during summer and russet-brown in autumn. If kept clipped, it will retain its dead leaves until the next spring.
GROWTH RATE: reaches 3–4ft (90–120cm) in 3 years and 6–8ft (1.8–2.4m) in 6 years.
PLANTING: set 18–24in (45–60cm) apart, from autumn to spring, in a sunny position.
SHAPING: leave the main stem unpruned for two years, lightly pruning any over-long or weak side shoots in the summer. Thereafter, clip to shape in mid-summer.

ILEX AQUIFOLIUM
(common or English holly)

Evergreen, hardy and tolerant plant which makes a spiny hedge. The species has glossy dark green leaves but there are many variegated cultivars. When clipped regularly, leaves are produced down to ground level.
GROWTH RATE: reaches 3–4ft (90–120cm) in 3 years and 6–8ft (1.8–2.4m) in 6 years.
PLANTING: set 18–24in (45–60cm) apart, in early autumn or late spring, in sun or light shade (non-variegated types tolerate dense shade).
SHAPING: use secateurs (hand pruners) to shape in spring or late summer.

PRUNUS LUSITANICA
(Portugal or bay laurel)

Evergreen and hardy with glossy dark green leaves, it makes a dense hedge if well pruned. It can be easily trained to form a small mophead or umbrella-shaped tree.
GROWTH RATE: reaches 4ft (120cm) in 3 yrs and 6–8ft (1.8–2.4m) in 6–8 yrs.
PLANTING: set 2ft (60cm) apart, in autumn or spring, in sun or light shade.
SHAPING: trim with secateurs (hand pruners) in spring and summer.

PYRACANTHA (firethorn)

Evergreen, hardy and tolerant, it bears white flowers in the early summer and yellow, orange or red berries in the autumn. It can be trained as an espalier but well-clipped, forms a dense, thorny hedge.
GROWTH RATE: reaches 3–4ft (90–120cm in 3 years and 6–8ft (1.8–2.4m) in 6 years, more if trained against a wall.
PLANTING: set 2ft (60cm) apart, in autumn or spring, in sun or light shade.
SHAPING: clip to shape any time from spring to early autumn. If fruit is required, trim after flowering.

SANTOLINA CHAMAECYPARISSUS
(cotton lavender)

Evergreen, low-growing shrub with feathery, aromatic, felted silver-grey foliage. If left unpruned, it produces yellow flowers in mid-summer, but these cause the foliage to become duller, and ruin the neat shape of a hedge.
GROWTH RATE: reaches 12–18in (30–45cm) in 2 years; it generally needs replacing after 6–8 years.
PLANTING: set 6–9in (15–20cm) apart, in spring, in a sunny position.
SHAPING: clip in spring and again during the summer.

CARPINUS BETULUS
(hornbeam)
Deciduous tolerant tree that makes a dense hedge which, if it is formally clipped, retains its russet-brown dead leaves until the next spring.
GROWTH RATE: reaches 4ft (120cm) in 4–5 years and 12ft (3–4m) in 8 years.
PLANTING: for hedges, set 18–24in (45–60cm) apart; for pleaching and stilt hedges, set 6–10ft (1.8–3m) apart, form autumn to spring, in sun or light shade.
SHAPING: leave the main stem unpruned for two years, lightly pruning any over-long or weak side shoots in the summer. Thereafter, clip to shape in summer.

CHAMAECYPARIS LAWSONIANA
Evergreen, hardy fast-growing conifer, of which the best cultivars are C.l. 'Allumii' with blue-grey foliage, and C.l. 'Green Hedges' with rich green foliage which makes a particularly hardy dense hedge.
PLANTING: 18–24in (45–60cm) apart, in mid-autumn or early spring, in a sunny position.
GROWTH RATE: reaches 5–6ft (1.5–1.8m) in 3 years and 8–10ft (2.5–3m) in 6–7 years.
SHAPING: trim in late spring and again during the summer as necessary.

CRATEAGUS MONOGYNA
(common or English hawthorn)
Deciduous, hardy, vigorous and tolerant shrub which makes an impenetrable thorny hedge. It responds well to hard clipping and can be pruned to form a mophead.
GROWTH RATE: reaches 3ft (90cm) in 3 years and 10–12ft (3–3.2m) in 10 years.
PLANTING: for hedges, set 12–15in (30–35cm) apart, in autumn to spring, in sun or light shade.
SHAPING: cut back to 6in (15cm) immediately after planting, and by one half of its growth the following winter. Thereafter, trim between early summer and autumn as necessary.

LAVANDULA ANGUSTIFOLIA
(old English lavender)
Evergreen, bushy, fragrant plant with silver-grey leaves and mauve-blue flowers in summer. The most compact forms are L.a. 'Hidcote' and L.a. 'Munstead Dwarf'.
GROWTH RATE: L.a. 'Hidcote' reaches its full height of 12–15in (30–40cm) in the second year, and L.a. 'Munstead Dwarf' reaches its full height of 2ft (60cm) in 2–3 years.
PLANTING: set L.a. 'Hidcote' 12in (30cm) apart, and L.a. 'Munstead Dwarf' 15in (35cm) apart, in autumn or late spring, in full sun.
SHAPING: clip in spring and immediately after flowering.

LIGUSTRUM OVALIFOLIUM (oval-leaved, common Japanese or Californian privet)
Semi-evergreen, but seldom without leaves, tolerant and vigorous enough to withstand frequent hard clipping. L.o. 'Aureum' is the golden privet with yellow variegated leaves.
GROWTH RATE: reaches 3ft (90cm) in 3 years and about 6ft (1.8m) in 6 years.
PLANTING: set 12–18in (30–45cm) apart, from autumn to spring, in sun or light shade.
SHAPING: cut back to 6in (15cm) immediately after planting and cut growth by one half the following winter to promote good foliage at the base. Thereafter, trim during the summer as necessary.

LONICERA NITIDA
(box-leaf honeysuckle)
Evergreen and fast-growing with small dark green leaves which resemble box, it forms a neat hedge if kept closely clipped. L.a. 'Baggesen's Gold' is also densely bushy with tiny rounded leaves which are golden all summer and turn pale green-yellow in the autumn.
GROWTH RATE: reaches 4ft (120cm) in 4 years and is best kept to this height.
PLANTING: set 9–12in (30cm) apart, from autumn to spring, in sun or light shade.
SHAPING: keep well battered to encourage foliage at the base; trim in spring and summer as necessary.

TAXUS BACCATA
(common or English yew)
Evergreen, hardy conifer with dense, very dark green foliage. The classic plant for topiary and ornamental hedges, it responds well to clipping and hard pruning.
GROWTH RATE: if well-fertilized, yew reaches 3ft (90cm) in 3 years, and then will grow 12–18in (30–45cm) a year to about 20ft (6m).
PLANTING: set 18–24in (45–60cm) apart, in autumn to spring, in sun or shade.
SHAPING: clip any long or straggly shoots immediately after planting. Thereafter, clip annually, in late summer.

TEUCRIUM CHAMAEDRYS
(germander)
Evergreen, hardy and aromatic dwarf shrub which makes a bushy hedge. The small oval toothed leaves are deep green above and grey beneath, giving an attractive appearance in the wind. Spikes of small pink flowers appear in mid summer.
GROWTH RATE: reaches 12–18in (30–45cm) in 3 years.
PLANTING: set 9in (25cm) apart in autumn or spring, in a sunny position.
SHAPING: trim once or twice in summer to maintain shape.

THUJA PLICATA
(western red cedar)
Evergreen, hardy, fast-growing conifer with dark green shiny scented foliage. With regular clipping it forms a dense hedge.
GROWTH RATE: reaches 5ft (1.5m) in 3 years and 8ft (2.5m) in 6 years and will grow to 15ft (4.5m) or more.
PLANTING: set 24–30in (60–80cm) apart, in autumn or spring, in a sunny position.
SHAPING: trim side shoots of young plants to encourage density, but do not cut off leader until intended height is reached. Thereafter, trim in late spring.

SHAPING HEDGES

Many evergreens, including box, conifers, holly and laurel should be treated this way:

After planting, trim straggly side shoots, but leave leader uncut. The following summer, prune side shoots to begin shaping sloping sides.

In the second and subsequent summers, trim side growth to maintain shape. Cut off the leader at the intended height of the hedge.

Some deciduous shrubs, including beech and hornbeam, should be treated this way:

After planting, lightly trim over-long or weak side shoots, but leave the leader unpruned for two years.

During the third and subsequent summers, cut back side growth to required shape and prune back main stem to encourage bushy growth.

Some fast-growing shrubs, including haw-thorn and privet, should be treated this way:

Immediately after planting, cut back plants to 6in (15cm) from the ground. This ensures that the base develops good bushy growth.

During the second winter, cut back the previous season's growth by at least one half. Then clip to maintain shape in summer.

BATTERING A HEDGE

Battering, or clipping a hedge to give an incline, improves its appearance and encourages growth at the base. A device with an adjustable arm can measure the correct incline of 2–4 in per foot (15–30cm per metre).

CLIPPING A HEDGE HORIZONTALLY

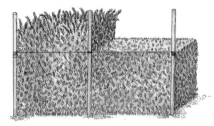

To check a continuous level, place stakes at about 6ft (1m) intervals, measure from the ground up to the desired height on each and clip along a string guideline tied at that level.

SCALLOPING A HEDGE

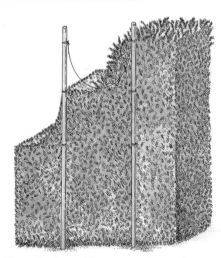

Use string looped between stakes as the guideline for full or half scallops; the string can be tied at varying heights as long as the stakes are placed at even intervals.

LAYING OUT A PARTERRE OR KNOT

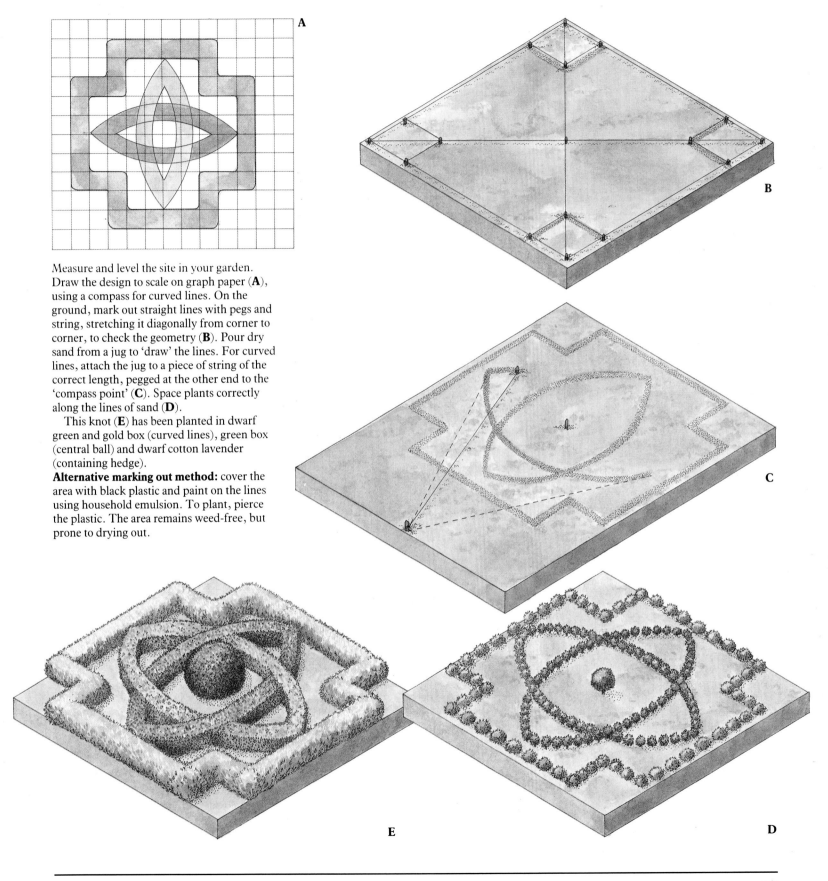

Measure and level the site in your garden. Draw the design to scale on graph paper (**A**), using a compass for curved lines. On the ground, mark out straight lines with pegs and string, stretching it diagonally from corner to corner, to check the geometry (**B**). Pour dry sand from a jug to 'draw' the lines. For curved lines, attach the jug to a piece of string of the correct length, pegged at the other end to the 'compass point' (**C**). Space plants correctly along the lines of sand (**D**).

This knot (**E**) has been planted in dwarf green and gold box (curved lines), green box (central ball) and dwarf cotton lavender (containing hedge).

Alternative marking out method: cover the area with black plastic and paint on the lines using household emulsion. To plant, pierce the plastic. The area remains weed-free, but prone to drying out.

TOPIARY AND TRAINING

TRAINING A MOPHEAD

In the first winter, tie the leader (main shoot or stem) of a speciment plant to a firm stake and trim most of the lateral (side) shoots to 2–3 in (5–7cm) long.

In the second winter, cut off the shortened laterals and trim new laterals to 2–3in (5–7cm). Continue pruning in this way as the tree grows.

Cut off the leader when it reaches the height of the centre of the intended mophead and allow new laterals to develop, pinching them out to encourage bushy growth.

To form an umbrella-shaped tree, train as for a mophead, but trim to a broader, semi-spherical shape once the head is formed.

MAKING A BALL ON TOP OF A SPHERE

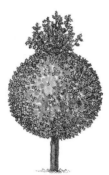

Prune and train the first sphere as a short-stemmed mophead, but do not cut off the leader (main shoot). Allow it to grow

into the stem or trunk of another smaller sphere, pruning it and cutting off the leader as for a mophead.

MAKING A SIMPLE SPIRAL

Drive a stake into the ground by the stem of a young supple conifer. Wind the plant round the stake, tying as necessary.

MAKING AN IVY SPIRAL

Push a cane into the ground close to the stem of a small-leaved ivy. Form a spiral from sturdy wire and attach to top and base of cane.

MAKING A PYRAMID OR OBELISK

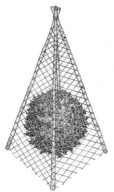

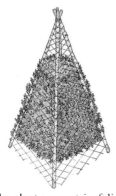

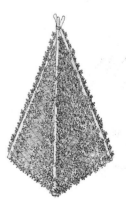

Place a frame of wire mesh and bamboo made to the intended size and shape around a plant made bushy from early pruning.

As the plant grows, trim foliage flush with the frame of the wire mesh.

Once the shape is formed, you can remove the frame or keep it hidden by the foliage and use it as a trimming guide.

To make a finial ball, leave leader to grow to central point of planned ball, then pinch out for bushy growth and trim to shape.

152

MAKING A 'CAKE STAND'

When the plant's base is almost the diameter of the first tier, clip horizontally. Trim the edge to an even radius using string attached to the stem as a compass.

Trim enough side shoots to leave a bare section of stem above the first tier. Train the second tier by tying down sideshoots to give a horizontal top surface.

Trim the second tier to a slightly smaller circle than the first. Develop a succession of tiers in the same way, keeping each one well clipped.

Form a ball at the top of the stand by pinching out the leader at the height of the centre of the intended sphere and prune as for a mophead.

MAKING A BIRD

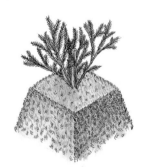   

When the base shape, such as an obelisk, is established, allow some strong shoots to grow about 18in-2ft (45–60cm) out from the centre of the top.

Push a stake through the base and tie it to the main stem. Form a simple outline frame from strong wire attached to the stake and tie in the shoots.

As you train the shoots around the frame, clip any that grow out of the shape to encourage bushier growth inside it. Keep clipping closely, improving the outline.

A dense shape will become apparent in about three years. This method can be used for any topiary shape, whether a finial or a container-grown specimen.

TRAINING A PLEACHED LIME AVENUE

Plant young standard trees at regular intervals of about 9-10ft (3m) in a line and secure their stems to a firm stake. Tie the

lateral braches into a framework of bamboo canes lashed to the stake on a single horizontal plane. Cut off leaders at the

desired height and train branches horizontally along the canes, trimming shoots that grow at the wrong angle to the frame.

Stilt hedges are initially trained in the same way as pleached trees, but are allowed to expand to a greater depth.

TRAINING FRUIT TREES

ESPALIER APPLE AND PEAR TREES

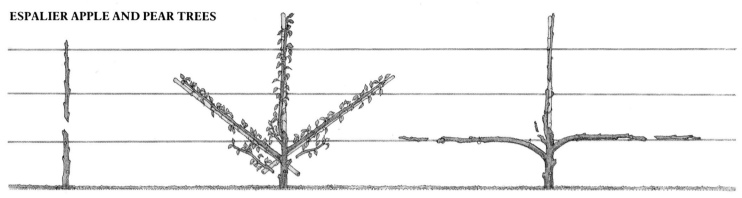

In the **first winter,** cut back to about 15in (35cm), ensuring that at least three good buds (nodes from which new shoots will grow) are left.

In the **following summer,** train the shoot from the top bud up a vertical cane and the laterals (side shoots) pointing outward along canes at 45°.

Early in the **second winter,** lower and tie the two trained laterals to the first horizontal wire support and shorten any other side shoots to two or three buds. Cut the vertical leader back within 18in (45cm) of the lower horizontal laterals, leaving three good buds from which the next tier of vertical leader and two main laterals will grow.

CORDON APPLE AND PEAR TREES

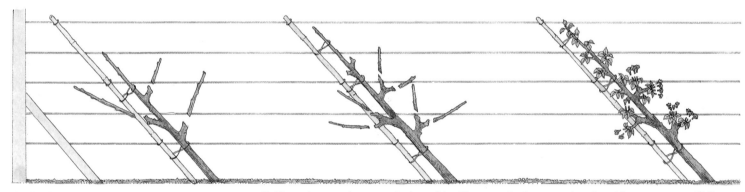

In the **first winter,** as soon as the tree is planted, cut back any laterals (side shoots) over 4in (10cm) long to leave three buds. Leave the leader unpruned.

Sublaterals (new shoots on the laterals) will have formed by the **second winter.** These should be cut back to two buds, but the leader should be left unpruned.

In the **second spring,** blossom spurs will form on the laterals. Cut off the flower buds as they appear, but do not cut the growing shoots behind the flowers.

FAN-TRAINED CHERRY TREE

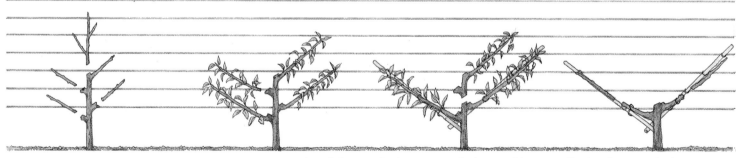

In the **first winter,** cut back the tree to a lateral (side shoot) at a height of about 24in (60cm). Leave this unpruned but shorten all laterals below it to one bud.

In the **following late spring,** tie in the top upward-pointing lateral and two more, the strongest one on each side pointing outward at 45°. Cut off all other laterals.

In **the summer** tie the two side (outward) laterals to canes. The upper lateral is left only to build up a strong plant. Later in the summer, it needs to be cut out.

During the **second winter,** prune the two side laterals to about 18in (45cm) each, cutting back to a strong bud, leaving a small, but strong, plant.

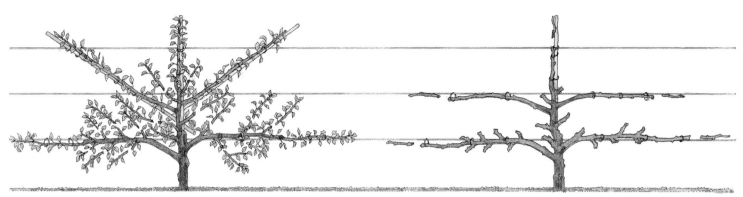

The **following summer,** train the second tier of laterals along canes at 45° and the leader further up the vertical cane. Cut back any other side shoots to three leaves, and any sublaterals (new shoots from the lateral branches) to three leaves from their basal cluster.

Early in the **third winter,** tie the second tier of laterals to the wire supports. Repeat the pruning of the leader to within about 18in (45cm) of the previous tier, again leaving three good buds. Tie extension growth on the first tier of laterals to the horizontal support and cut back any surplus side shoots to three buds.

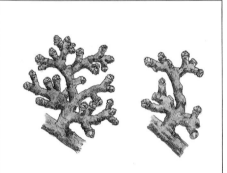

Late in the **second summer,** cut back laterals longer than 8in (20cm) to leave three leaves and cut back sublaterals to leave one leaf above their basal clusters.

Once the leader reaches the required height, it should be cut back at the same time as the summer or winter pruning of the laterals to about 1in (3cm) above the topmost lateral.

As the tree matures, thin out by reducing overcrowded and complicated spur systems, removing buds which are weak or in the shaded parts of the branches.

Next summer, tie in four of the sublaterals (new shoots) on each side lateral — two above, one below and one extension. Cut back all other shoots to one leaf.

In the **third winter,** shorten each of the four trained sublaterals on each side by about a third, cutting each one back to a downward facing bud.

In the **following summer,** tie in three new shoots from each of the eight sub-laterals and, later, pinch out the shoots which arise from them at 18in (45cm).

In the subsequent years, after harvesting the fruit in late summer, cut back the laterals that have fruited to the young replacement shoots.

INDEX

FURTHER READING

I do little here but list those books in English either in print or reasonably easily available from a library which the reader who wishes to pursue the subject of formal gardens further may find of use.

GARDEN HISTORY

ADAMS, William Howard, *The French Garden 1500–1800*, New York and London, 1979

BLOMFIELD, Reginald, and THOMAS, F. Inigo, *The Formal Garden in England*, London, 1982

CASA VALDES, Marquesa de, *Spanish Gardens*, Antique Collector's Club, 1987

COFFIN, David R., *The Villa in the Life of Renaissance Rome*, Princeton U.P., 1979

ELLIOTT, Brent, *Victorian Gardens*, London, 1986

GOTHEIN, Marie Luise, *A History of Garden Art*, London, 1928

HADFIELD, Miles, *A History of British Gardening*, London, 1960

HARRIS, John, *The Artist and the Country House*, London, 1979

HAZELHURST, F. Hamilton, *Gardens of Illusion: The Genius of André Le Nostre*, Vanderbilt U.P., 1980

JACQUES, David and HORST, Arend van der, *The Gardens of William and Mary*, London, 1988

JEKYLL Gertrude, and WEAVER, Lawrence, *Gardens for Small Country Houses*, London, 1920 ed.

JOURNAL OF GARDEN HISTORY VIII, no. 2–3, 1988. *The Anglo-Dutch Garden in the Age of William and Mary*

MACDOUGALL, Elisabeth B., and HAZLEHURST, F. Hamilton, *The French Formal Garden*, Dumbarton Oaks Colloquium on the History of Landscape Architecture, Dumbarton Oaks, 1974

MASSON, Georgina, *Italian Gardens*, London, 1961

SHEPHERD, J.C. and JELLICOE, G.A., *Italian Renaissance Gardens*, London, 1986 ed.

STRONG, Roy, *The Renaissance Garden in England*, London, 1979

TRIGGS, H. Inigo, *Formal Gardens in England and Scotland*, London, 1902

WOODBRIDGE, Kenneth, *Princely Gardens. The Origins and Development of the French Formal Style*, London, 1986

DESIGN

BALSTON, Michael, *The Well-Furnished Garden*, London, 1986

HICKS, David, *Garden Design*, London, 1982

SWANSON, Faith H., and RADY, Virginia B., *Herb Garden Design*, University Press of New England, 1984

VEREY, Rosemary, *Classic Garden Design. How to adapt and recreate garden features of the past*, London, 1984

TOPIARY AND TRAINING

CLEVELY, A. M. *Topiary. The Art of Clipping Trees and Ornamental Hedges*, London, 1988

HADFIELD, Miles, *Topiary and Ornamental Hedges*, London, 1971

LACEY, Geraldine, *Creating Topiary*, London 1987

LLOYD, Nathaniel, *Garden Craftsmanship in Yew and Box*, London, 1925

The Fruit Garden Displayed, Royal Horticultural Society, 1986

PLANT HISTORY

BUNYARD, Edward, *Old Garden Roses*, London, 1936

STUART, David, and SUTHERLAND, James, *Plants from the Past. Old Flowers for New Gardens*, London, 1987

THOMAS, Graham Stuart, *The Old Shrub Roses*, London, 1961

ACKNOWLEDGMENTS

The publisher would like to thank the following photographers and organizations for their kind permission to reproduce the photographs in this book:

1–3 Gary Rogers; 5 Marijke Heuff (Mr & Mrs Jaap Nieuwenhuis and Paula Thies); 6 Andrew Lawson; 7 Philippe Perdereau; 8–9 Marijke Heuff (Mr & Mrs Jaap Nieuwenhuis and Paula Thies); 10–11 Clive Boursnell; 11 Georges Lévêque; 12 Marijke Heuff (Mr & Mrs Martin Lane Fox, Hazelby House); 13 Jerry Harpur; 14 Marijke Heuff; 15 above Marijke Heuff (Mrs Greve-Verhaar); 15 below Jerry Harpur (Liz Longhurst, Killara, Sydney); 16–17 Marijke Heuff (designer Mr K T Noordhuis); 17 Marijke Heuff (Mr & Mrs Jaap Nieuwenhuis and Paula Thies); 18 above left Georges Lévêque (Patricia van Roosmalen); 18 above right Marijke Heuff (de Walenburg); 18 below Marijke Heuff; 19 above Marijke Heuff (Barnsley House); 19 below Marijke Heuff; 20 above Marijke Heuff (Mr & Mrs ter Kuile Nijpels); 20 below Andrew Lawson (Roy Strong); 21 left Eric Crichton (Major and Mrs Mordaunt-Hare, Fitz House); 21 right Lamontagne; 22 above Georges Lévêque; 22 below Eric Crichton (Lord and Lady Carrington, The Manor House, Bedlow); 23 above Marijke Heuff (designer Jacques Wirtz); 23 below left Georges Lévêque; 23 below right Marijke Heuff (Mr & Mrs Dekker-Fokker); 24 Lamontagne; 25 above left Philippe Perdereau; 25 above right Lamontagne; 25 below left Hugh Palmer; 25 below right Karen Bussolini; 52 Marijke Heuff (Mr & Mrs Martin Lane Fox, Hazelby House); 53 Marijke Heuff (Mr & Mrs de la Hayze); 54 Andrew Lawson; 55 Gary Rogers; 56 Tassa Traeger; 56–57 Clive Boursnell; 57 above Georges Lévêque; 57 below Jerry Harpur (Tradescant Trust); 58 above left Lamontagne; 58 below left Hugh Palmer; 58 above right Gary Rogers; 58 below right Hugh Palmer (Tudor Garden, Southampton); 59 above left Marijke Heuff; 59 below left Jerry Harpur; 59 above right Clay Perry; 59 below right Marijke Heuff (Huis te Jaarsveld); 60–61 Marijke Heuff (Zaanse Schans); 62 Andrew Lawson; 63 Marijke Heuff (Sparrendaal); 64 above Clive Boursnell; 64 below Jerry Harpur; 65 Jerry Harpur (Westbury Court); 66 Marijke Heuff (Patricia van Roosmalen); 67 above Marijke Heuff (Castle Warmelo); 67 centre Marijke Heuff (Nymans); 67 below left Marijke Heuff (Hidcote); 67 below right Marijke Heuff (Patricia van Roosmalen); 68 Marijke Heuff (Mr & Mrs Dekker-Fokker); 69 Karl Dietrich Buhler/Elizabeth Whiting & Associates; 70 above Hugh Palmer; 70 below Marijke Heuff; 71 above Georges Lévêque; 71 below Georges Lévêque; 72 above Georges Lévêque (designer Jacques Wirtz); 72 below left Marijke Heuff (designer Piet Blanckaert); 72 below right Marijke Heuff (designer Piet Blanckaert); 73 Georges Lévêque (designer Jacques Wirtz); 74 Marijke Heuff (Hever Castle); 75 Hugh Palmer (Saling Hall); 76–77 Georges Lévêque; 78–79 Marijke Heuff (Mr & Mrs Jaap Nieuwenhuis and Paula Thies); 79 Lamontagne; 80 Eric Crichton (Lady Heald, Chilworth Manor); 81 Eric Crichton (Mr & Mrs Paul Hobhouse, Hadspen House); 82 Marijke Heuff (Garden at Castle van Sypesteyn at Nieuw-Loosdrecht); 83 Marijke Heuff (Patricia van Roosmalen); 84 Hugh Palmer (Kellie Castle); 85 above Jerry Harpur (Abbotswood, Stow-on-the Wold); 85 below Jerry Harpur (Mains of Edzell); 86 above Gary Rogers; 86 below Marijke Heuff (Patricia van Roosmalen); 87 Marijke Heuff; 88 The World of Interiors/James Mortimer; 89 Marijke Heuff (Mr & Mrs de la Hayze); 90 above Marijke Heuff (Patricia van Roosmalen); 90 below left Georges Lévêque (designer Jacques Wirtz); 90 below right Georges Lévêque; 91 Lamontagne; 92 Clay Perry; 93 Marijke Heuff (Barnsley House); 94 Georges Lévêque; 95 above Eric Crichton (Emmanuel College, Cambridge); 95 below Clay Perry; 96 Marijke Heuff; 97 Lamontagne; 98 left Lamontagne; 98 right Gary Rogers; 99 Georges Lévêque; 100–101 Marijke Heuff; 101 above Marijke Heuff (Barnsley House); 101 below Marijke Heuffe (Mr & Mrs van Bennekom).